ANNE OF GREEN GABLES

A Musical in Two Acts

From the novel by
L.M. MONTGOMERY

Book by
JOSEPH ROBINETTE

Music and Lyrics by
EVELYN D. SWENSSON

Dramatic Publishing
Woodstock, Illinois • London, England • Melbourne, Australia

*** NOTICE ***

The amateur and stock acting rights to this work are controlled exclusively by THE DRAMATIC PUBLISHING COMPANY without whose permission in writing no performance of it may be given. Royalty fees are given in our current catalog and are subject to change without notice. Royalty must be paid every time a play is performed whether or not it is presented for profit and whether or not admission is charged. A play is performed any time it is acted before an audience. All inquiries concerning amateur and stock rights should be addressed to:

DRAMATIC PUBLISHING
P. O. Box 129, Woodstock, Illinois 60098

COPYRIGHT LAW GIVES THE AUTHOR OR THE AUTHOR'S AGENT THE EXCLUSIVE RIGHT TO MAKE COPIES. This law provides authors with a fair return for their creative efforts. Authors earn their living from the royalties they receive from book sales and from the performance of their work. Conscientious observance of copyright law is not only ethical, it encourages authors to continue their creative work. This work is fully protected by copyright. No alterations, deletions or substitutions may be made in the work without the prior written consent of the publisher. No part of this work may be reproduced or transmitted in any form or by any means, electronic or mechanical, including photocopy, recording, videotape, film, or any information storage and retrieval system, without permission in writing from the publisher. It may not be performed either by professionals or amateurs without payment of royalty. All rights, including but not limited to the professional, motion picture, radio, television, videotape, foreign language, tabloid, recitation, lecturing, publication, and reading are reserved. *On all programs this notice should appear:*

"Produced by special arrangement with
THE DRAMATIC PUBLISHING COMPANY of Woodstock, Illinois"

©MCMXCVII
Book by
JOSEPH ROBINETTE
Music and Lyrics by
EVELYN D. SWENSSON

From the novel by
L.M. MONTGOMERY

Printed in the United States of America
All Rights Reserved
(ANNE OF GREEN GABLES)

Cover design by Susan Carle

ISBN 0-87129-760-4

ANNE OF GREEN GABLES

A Musical in Two Acts
For 6-12 Men and 12-18 Women, and Extras if desired

CHARACTERS

ANNE SHIRLEY	RUBY GILLIS
MATTHEW CUTHBERT	JIMMY GLOVER
MARILLA CUTHBERT	MOODY MACPHERSON
RACHEL LYNDE	CHARLIE SLOANE
MR. PHILLIPS	JANE ANDREWS
PRISSY ANDREWS	GILBERT BLYTHE
DIANA BARRY	MISS SUSAN STACY
MRS. BARRY	AUNT JOSEPHINE BARRY
MINNIE MAY BARRY	MRS. ALLAN
JOSIE PYE	

Minor speaking roles

STATIONMASTER	REVEREND BENTLEY
MISS ROGERSON	TILLIE BOULTER
BESSIE WRIGHT	MARY JO
REVEREND ALLAN	CARRIE SLOANE
PROFESSOR ENGERRAND	PRES. OF QUEEN'S ACADEMY
MR. SADLER	

<u>EXTRAS</u>: Schoolchildren, Girls and Boys at Sunday School, Graduates of Queen's Academy, Townspeople. (All extras may be cast from the actors playing minor speaking roles.)

THE TIME: The early 1900s.
THE PLACE: Avonlea,
and other locations on Prince Edward Island, Canada.

******

ANNE OF GREEN GABLES premiered at Delaware Children's Theatre in Wilmington, Delaware, directed by Marie Swajeski.

Doubling Suggestions for a Cast of
6 Men and 12 Women

1ST ACTOR
Stationmaster
Mr. Phillips
Reverend Allan
Professor Engerrand

1ST ACTRESS
Tillie Boulter
Miss Susan Stacy
Carrie Sloane

2ND ACTOR
Charlie Sloane
Mr. Sadler

2ND ACTRESS
Prissy Andrews
Aunt Josephine Barry

3RD ACTOR
Reverend Bentley
Jimmy Glover
Pres. of Queen's Academy

3RD ACTRESS
Miss Rogerson
Bessie Wright
Mary Jo
Mrs. Allan

The following roles should not be double cast:

Anne Shirley
Matthew Cuthbert
Marilla Cuthbert
Rachel Lynde
Diana Barry
Mrs. Barry

Minnie May Barry
Josie Pye
Ruby Gillis
Moody MacPherson
Jane Andrews
Gilbert Blythe

VOCAL SELECTIONS

Act One

Prince Edward Island (Prologue) .... Townspeople
Where and Why .... Rachel & Marilla
Green Gables .... Anne
Jesus Loves Me/Have You Heard? .... Sunday School Pupils
The Pledge/Amazing Grace ... Anne & Diana, Offstage Choir
Kindred Spirits .... Anne & Diana
School Days .... Students
Farewell .... Anne & Diana
Anne of Green Gables .... Gilbert
God's in His Heaven ... Anne, Diana, Mary Jo, Offstage Choir

Act Two

Deck the Halls .... Carolers
Reprise: Kindred Spirits ...... Anne, Diana, Aunt Josephine
I Dare You! .... Students
Reprise: Anne of Green Gables ... Mrs. Allan, Marilla, Matthew
Marilla Regrets .... Marilla
The Charlottetown Rag ...Miss Stacy, Prof. Engerrand, Students
Pomp and Circumstance March .... Students
Shall We Gather at the River? .... Townspeople
My Little Girl .... Marilla
Curtain Calls (Anne Of Green Gables) .... Entire Cast

SYNOPSIS OF SCENES

ACT ONE

1. An Open Meadow (Prologue)
2. Train Station Platform
3. Green Gables (Kitchen/sitting room)
4. Street in Avonlea
5. Green Gables
6. Sunday School Classroom
7. Green Gables
8. Barry's Parlor
9. Schoolyard/Classroom
10. Green Gables
11. Barry's Parlor

ACT TWO

1. Green Gables
2. Barry's Parlor
3. Street in Avonlea
4. Barry's Parlor
5. Green Gables
6. Barry's Parlor/Queen's Academy Study Room
7. Green Gables
8. Boarding House Parlor at Queen's Academy
9. Street in Charlottetown
10. A Courtyard at Queen's Academy
11. Green Gables
12. Cemetery Road
13. Green Gables

PROLOGUE

SCENE: *An open meadow on Prince Edward Island, Canada.*

(MUSIC #1: "PRINCE EDWARD ISLAND")

(Offstage laughter and shouts are heard. Moments later, several young PEOPLE enter playing tag, hide-and-seek, etc. They are followed by slightly out-of-breath ADULTS who carry picnic baskets and blankets. The frivolity is punctuated by: "You're it," "Children, slow down," "You can't catch me," "Don't get dirty before the picnic even starts," etc. ALL begin to spread blankets and settle down as RACHEL LYNDE, mid-50s, enters with an unnecessary walking cane which she uses to point or to tap the ground for emphasis.)

RACHEL *(singing).*
    EAST OF MONTREAL, QUEBEC,
    AND NORTH OF PORTLAND, MAINE,
    THERE IS AN ISLAND WHICH IS PART OF
    CANADA'S DOMAIN.

ALL.
    PRINCE EDWARD ISLAND,
    THE GARDEN OF THE SEA.
    PRINCE EDWARD ISLAND,
    THE PLACE FOR YOU AND ME.

CHILDREN.
    THE SUNDAY SCHOOL HAS A PICNIC
    ON A SUNNY DAY IN MAY.
    WE'LL EAT ICE CREAM AND WIN A PRIZE
    IF WE WIN A RACE TODAY.

ALL.
> PRINCE EDWARD ISLAND,
> THE GARDEN OF THE SEA.
> PRINCE EDWARD ISLAND,
> THE PLACE FOR YOU AND ME.

WOMEN & TEEN GIRLS.
> THE ROLLING HILLS ARE LUSH AND GREEN.
> ST. LAWRENCE GULF IS BLUE.
> THE ROADS OF CLAY ARE RUSTY RED,
> THE SANDY BEACHES, TOO.

ALL.
> PRINCE EDWARD ISLAND,
> THE GARDEN OF THE SEA.
> PRINCE EDWARD ISLAND,
> THE PLACE FOR YOU AND ME.

RACHEL.
> I'M RACHEL LYNDE, THE MOTHER OF TWELVE—
> I MANAGE MY OWN AFFAIRS
> AND STILL HAVE TIME LEFT OVER
> TO HELP MY NEIGHBORS WITH THEIRS.

ALL.
> TO HELP HER NEIGHBORS WITH THEIRS.

RACHEL.
> I'M PRESIDENT OF EV'RYTHING—
> GOOD CAUSES I ESPOUSE.
> IN TRUTH, I WOULD DO ANYTHING
> TO GET ME OUT OF THE HOUSE.

ALL.
> TO GET HER OUT OF THE HOUSE.

RACHEL.
> I KNOW EVERYONE ON THE ISLAND,
> THEIR JOYS AND SORROWS AND SIN,
> SO LET ME INTRODUCE YOU
> TO MY NEIGHBORS AND THEIR KIN.

ALL.
> TO HER NEIGHBORS AND THEIR KIN.

RACHEL.
> THERE'S BEAUTIFUL MISSUS BARRY,
> DIANA AND YOUNG MINNIE MAY,
> REVEREND BENTLEY AND MISS ROGERSON—

REV. BENTLEY & MISS ROGERSON *(shaking their fingers at the CHILDREN).*
> YOU'D BETTER WATCH WHAT YOU SAY!

CHILDREN.
> WE'D BETTER WATCH WHAT WE SAY.
>
> *(They cover their mouths with their hands.)*

RACHEL.
> JOSIE PYE AND THE OTHER GIRLS
> ARE PLAYING A GAME OF "FREEZE."
> GILBERT BLYTHE AND THE OTHER BOYS
> ARE PLAYING A GAME OF "TEASE."

ALL.
> ARE PLAYING A GAME OF "TEASE."

RACHEL.
>MARILLA AND MATTHEW CUTHBERT
>ARE STANDIN' THERE IN THE SHADE.
>GREEN GABLES IS THEIR FARM HOUSE.
>HE'S A BACH'LOR; SHE'S AN OLD MAID.
>
>FROM BIRTH TO DEATH OUR LIVES ARE LIVED
>IN PATTERNS SIMPLE AND SLOW.
>GOD ONLY KNOW WHAT WILL HAPPEN
>BUT *IF* SOMETHING HAPPENS, AND *WHEN*
>>SOMETHING HAPPENS,

RACHEL & ALL.
>I'LL (SHE'LL) BE THE FIRST TO KNOW!

ALL.
>IF WE HAD A CHOICE,
>THERE'S NOWHERE ELSE WE'D RATHER BE
>THAN HERE WITH FRIENDS AND FAM'LIES
>IN THE TOWN OF AVONLEA ON—
>
>PRINCE EDWARD ISLAND,
>THE GARDEN OF THE SEA.
>PRINCE EDWARD ISLAND,
>THE PLACE FOR YOU AND ME...AND ME!

(Optional)

(MUSIC #1A: "PLAYOFF: PRINCE EDWARD ISLAND")

ALL *(as they exit).*
>PRINCE EDWARD ISLAND,
>THE PLACE FOR YOU AND ME!

ACT ONE

SCENE: *A platform at the Bright River train station. ANNE SHIRLEY, a young girl, sets her suitcase down and glances about nervously. She speaks as though rehearsing a presentation.*

ANNE. Hello, my name is Anne Shirley, but please call me Cordelia. I think Cordelia is a much better name for me, don't you think? I am truly honored and excited to be going to Green Gables with you, Mr. Cuthbert. I feel I'm the most fortunate girl in the whole universe... or at least in the whole dominion of Canada. *(She walks to the edge of the platform and continues "rehearsing.")* Hello, my name is Anne Shirley, but please call me Cordelia—

(Her voice trails off, but she continues to mouth the words as the STATIONMASTER and MATTHEW CUTHBERT, in his early 60s, enter. ANNE does not notice them.)

STATIONMASTER *(pointing to ANNE)*. There she is at the end of the platform.
MATTHEW. But it's a boy I've come for. Mrs. Spenser was to bring a boy over from Nova Scotia. Then I was to take him home to Avonlea.
STATIONMASTER. Well, Mrs. Spenser got off the train with that girl and left her in my charge till you got here.
MATTHEW. There must be some mistake.

STATIONMASTER. Maybe she can explain it. She sure is a talker, that one. Now, you'll excuse me, Matthew. That's the last train today, and I'm going home for my supper. *(He exits. MATTHEW walks tentatively toward ANNE who stops reciting to herself when she sees him.)*

ANNE. Oh. I do hope you are Mr. Matthew Cuthbert.

MATTHEW. Well now, I reckon that's me.

ANNE *(brightly, giving her "speech")*. Hello, my name is Anne Shirley, but please call me Cordelia. I think Cordelia is a much better—

MATTHEW. Yes, yes, I heard you saying all that a little earlier.

ANNE. I was beginning to be afraid you weren't coming for me. If you hadn't, I was going to climb that big cherry tree down the tracks and spend the night in it.

MATTHEW. You're not a boy.

ANNE. But I can climb all the same. And I wouldn't be the least bit afraid.

MATTHEW. Well now, I guess I can't leave you here. I'll take you home and see what Marilla says. The horse and buggy are over there. I'll carry your bag.

ANNE *(picking up the suitcase)*. Oh, I can manage it. All my worldly goods are in it, but it isn't heavy. Now isn't that beautiful?

MATTHEW. What?

ANNE. That tree over there. What does it make you think of?

MATTHEW. Well now, I dunno.

ANNE. A bride, of course, with a misty veil. I don't ever expect to be a bride myself. I'm so homely nobody would ever want to marry me—except maybe a foreign missionary. Am I talking too much? People are always telling me I do. Would you rather I didn't talk? *(Somewhat unexpectedly, MATTHEW finds himself becoming intrigued by the waif before him.)*

MATTHEW. Well now, I don't mind talkative folks so much since I'm kinda quiet myself. Talk as much as you like.

ANNE. Oh, thank you. I can already tell we're kindred spirits, Mr. Cuthbert. I can hardly wait to see Green Gables. It makes me almost perfectly happy. But I can never be *perfectly* happy because of this. *(She holds out one of her braids.)*

MATTHEW. Your hair?

ANNE. What color would you call it?

MATTHEW. Red, ain't it?

ANNE *(gloomily)*. Yes, red. I can imagine away my freckles and green eyes and skinniness—but not my red hair. Have you ever imagined what it would be like to be divinely beautiful, Mr. Cuthbert?

MATTHEW. Well now, no, I haven't.

ANNE. Will your sister like me even though I'm not divinely beautiful?

MATTHEW. I doubt that'd bother her much, but something else might. We'd better get home.

ANNE. Home! What a lovely sound—almost angelic. I don't know that I'll ever get used to it.

MATTHEW. Let's hope you get the chance. Come along now.

ANNE. Oh, yes. Let's not delay. *(They start to leave.)* Mrs. Spenser told me all about Green Gables, and it seems like a dream. I've pinched myself black and blue from the elbows up hoping it wasn't a dream. You see, Mr. Cuthbert, all my life—*(Her voice trails off as they exit.)*

(MUSIC #2: "WHERE AND WHY")

(The scene changes to the kitchen/sitting room of Green Gables. There is a knock at the door. MARILLA CUTHBERT, a woman in her mid-50s, enters from another part of the house.)

RACHEL'S VOICE *(offstage, singing).*
MARILLA! MARILLA!
MARILLA! MARILLA!

(MARILLA opens the door to reveal a breathless RACHEL.)

RACHEL.
I WAS SITTIN' AT THE WINDOW SHELLIN' PEAS
WHEN I SAW MATTHEW GO BY.
I HAVEN'T SEEN HIM COME BACK YET,
SO, OF COURSE, I WONDER WHY.

HE WAS ALL DRESSED UP IN HIS SUNDAY SUIT.
HE WAS DRIVIN' THE SORREL MARE.
HE WAS DRIVIN' OUT OF AVONLEA,
AND I CAN'T FIGURE OUT WHERE.

HE WAS DRIVIN' TOO SLOW FOR THE DOCTOR.
HE WAS TOO DRESSED UP FOR THE STORE.
HE'S WAY TOO SHY TO GO CALLIN',
SO WHAT WAS HE GOIN' FOR?

I HEARD HE WAS GOIN' TO PLANT TODAY.

MARILLA.
HE DID.

RACHEL.
AND?

MARILLA.
HE LEFT.

Act I ANNE OF GREEN GABLES Page 15

RACHEL.
> AND?
> NOT BEIN' THE NOSY TYPE,
> I CERTAINLY WON'T PRY,
> BUT I AM SURE THERE'S MORE TO THIS
> THAN MEETS THE NAKED EYE.

MARILLA *(speaking).* I suppose you might as well know. *(Singing.)*
> MATTHEW WENT TO BRIGHT RIVER.
> WE'RE GETTING A BOY TODAY—
> A BOY FROM THE ORPHAN ASYLUM.
> THEY SHOULD BE ON THEIR WAY.
>
> WON'T YOU HAVE SOME TEA?

RACHEL.
> NOT ME! MARILLA. HOW ILL-ADVISED!
> IF HE'D GONE TO AUSTRALIA FOR A KANGAROO
> I COULDN'T BE MORE SURPRISED!

(Speaking.) Are you really in earnest?

MARILLA. Yes, of course. We've been thinking about it for some time. *(Singing.)*
> MATTHEW'S HEART IS TROUBLING HIM.
> WE NEED A BOY ON THE FARM
> TO PLOW THE FIELDS AND DO THE CHORES
> AND KEEP THE SHEEP FROM HARM.

RACHEL.
> MARILLA! WHAT A FOOLISH THING!
> I NEED TO TELL YOU PLAIN—

> **TO TAKE A STRANGER UNDER YOUR WING**
> **IS TOTALLY INSANE.**
>
> **JUST LAST WEEK I READ ABOUT**
> **AN ORPHAN BOY FOR HIRE.**
> **A FAMILY TOOK HIM IN—**
>
> *(Speaking.)* Guess what?
> *(Singing.)*
>
> **HE SET THEIR HOUSE ON FIRE!**
>
> *(Speaking.)* On purpose!
> *(Singing.)*
>
> **ANOTHER ONE I HEARD ABOUT**
>
> *(Speaking.)* Put poison down the well.
> *(Singing.)*
>
> **THAT ONE WAS A GIRL, THOUGH,**
> **A WICKED JEZEBEL!**

MARILLA *(speaking)*. Well, we're not getting a girl. Matthew's afraid of them, and I'd never dream of bringing one up.

RACHEL. Well, I can't wait to tell—*(Correcting herself.)*—to *see* how all this comes out. *(A horse whinny is heard outside. RACHEL goes to the window.)* Look, there's Matthew and the boy pulling up now. Hard to see him in this light, but looks like the first thing you're going to have to do is give him a haircut. I'll just slip out the side door so you and Matthew can be alone with the new boy. *(She starts to leave.)* Oh, and Marilla—if I were you, I'd keep the lid fastened real tight over the well. *(She exits.)*

ANNE'S VOICE *(offstage)*. The drive here was so pretty! No, that's not the right word. Nor beautiful, either. It was wonderful...wonderful!

(ANNE and MATTHEW enter.)

ANNE *(seeing MARILLA)*. Oh...hello. You must be—
MARILLA. Matthew Cuthbert, who's that? Where's the boy?
MATTHEW. There wasn't any boy. There was only her.
MARILLA. We asked for a boy. Why did you bring her?
MATTHEW. I couldn't leave her at the station, no matter how the mistake came to be.
MARILLA *(glaring at ANNE)*. Well, this is a pretty piece of business.
ANNE *(after a pause)*. You don't want me? You don't want me because I'm not a boy? *(Near tears.)* I might have expected it. Nobody ever wanted me. I might have known it was too beautiful to last. *(She cries.)*
MARILLA. Well, well, there's no need to cry about it.
ANNE. Yes, there is. You'd cry, too, if you were an orphan and had come to a place you thought was home but wasn't because you weren't a boy. *(MATTHEW offers her a handkerchief which she blows into, then returns to him. MARILLA finds herself slightly amused, revealing the hint of a smile.)*
MARILLA. Well, don't cry anymore. We're not going to turn you out of doors tonight. What's your name?
ANNE *(pulling herself together and "reciting")*. My name is Anne Shirley, but please call me Cordelia. I think Cordelia is a much better—
MARILLA. What's wrong with calling you by your real name?
ANNE. It's so unromantic.
MARILLA. Fiddlesticks. It's a good, sensible name.
ANNE. Very well. If you must call me Anne, please call me Anne spelled with an "e" at the end.

MARILLA. All right—Anne with an "e"—can you tell us how this mistake came to be? Were there no boys at the orphan asylum?

ANNE. Oh, yes, but Mrs. Spenser thought you wanted a girl...Oh, Mr. Cuthbert, why didn't you tell me at the station you didn't want me and leave me there?

MATTHEW. Well now, I—

ANNE. If I hadn't seen the White Way of Delight and the Lake of Shining Waters, it wouldn't be quite so hard to leave.

MARILLA. What on earth does she mean?

MATTHEW. It's new names she gave to the apple tree grove and Barry's pond.

MARILLA. Sounds like your imagination works overtime. Come upstairs, and I'll show you where you can sleep tonight. Then we'll have some supper.

ANNE. I won't have any, thank you. I can't eat when I'm in the depths of despair. Can you?

MARILLA. I've never been in the depths of despair, so I can't say.

ANNE. You could imagine what it would be like.

MARILLA. I've got my hands full handling the *real* things in life. I got no time for imagination. Come on. *(She and ANNE exit in the direction of the upstairs. MATTHEW appears somewhat agitated. He takes a pipe and tobacco from a drawer.)*

(MARILLA re-enters, calling back upstairs.)

MARILLA. You can unpack your things first, then come back down. If you still don't want any supper, you can at least say good night. *(To MATTHEW.)* We'll send her back to the orphan asylum tomorrow.

MATTHEW. Well now, I—

MARILLA. Matthew Cuthbert, you never take out that pipe unless something's weighing on your mind. What is it?

MATTHEW. I was just thinking it seems a kind of pity to send her back when she's so set on staying here.

MARILLA. You mean to say you think we ought to keep her?

MATTHEW. She's a real nice little thing. Real interesting, too. *(A slight chuckle.)*

MARILLA. You need somebody to help you with the chores.

MATTHEW. I could hire a local boy part-time. The girl could be company for you.

MARILLA. I'm not suffering for company. And I don't aim to keep her. And I wish you'd go outside with that pipe.

MATTHEW. I'll put the mare in the barn. *(He exits.)*

(MARILLA paces uncomfortably as ANNE enters.)

ANNE. Oh, Miss Cuthbert, I love the view from the window upstairs. In the moonlight, the trees and flowers are fairly shimmering. They seemed to be calling me, "Anne, Anne, come out to us. We need a playmate." But I don't dare go out, of course. There's no use in loving things if you have to be torn from them, is there?

MARILLA *(after a pause)*. Can you do chores?

ANNE. Oh, yes. I can sweep and clean and wash dishes—

MARILLA. I mean outside chores...Oh, never mind. That Matthew—what's he got me thinking? He's a ridiculous man.

ANNE. I think he's lovely. He didn't mind how much I talked. The moment I saw him, I felt we were kindred spirits.

MARILLA. You're both kinda strange, if that's what you mean by kindred spirits.

ANNE. Oh, Miss Cuthbert, please let me stay here. I'll do anything you ask.

MARILLA. Well, you might start by going upstairs and getting dressed for bed. And don't forget to say your prayers.

ANNE. I don't know how.

MARILLA. You've never been taught to say prayers? You love God, don't you?

ANNE. Well...He gave me red hair, so I never cared for Him very much.

MARILLA. Young lady! I can see you need some strong religious training, and we'll start right now with your prayers. Kneel down here with me. *(She and ANNE kneel.)* Thank God for his blessings and ask him humbly for the things you want.

ANNE. Okay. *(Praying.)* Dear Father, I thank thee for the White Way of Delight and the Lake of Shining Waters. And that's all the blessings I can think of right now.

(MATTHEW enters. MARILLA motions for him to be quiet.)

ANNE. As for the things I want, they're so numerous, I will only mention the two most important. Please, *please* let me stay at Green Gables. And please let me be good looking when I grow up. I remain, yours respectfully, Anne Shirley. That's Anne with an "e." *(To MARILLA.)* Good-night. *(She exits toward the upstairs.)*

MARILLA *(after a long pause)*. I've never brought up a child before—especially a girl. And I'll probably make a terrible mess of it. But it's about time somebody adopted that child and taught her something. As far as I'm concerned, Matthew, she can stay.

MATTHEW *(pleased, as he puts his pipe away)*. Well now...

Act I   ANNE OF GREEN GABLES   Page 21

MARILLA. I'll try to make her useful and train her properly, but don't you go interfering with my methods. I suppose an old maid knows more about bringing up a child than an old bachelor. *(A horse whinny is heard outside.)* I thought you put the mare away.

MATTHEW. Guess I had my mind on that little girl so much, I plumb forgot.

MARILLA. Looks like I've got *two* children to look after instead of one. Come on. You unhitch the wagon, and I'll put up the mare. *(They exit.)*

(MUSIC #3: "GREEN GABLES")

(A light comes up on ANNE, now in a nightgown, looking out her bedroom window—or she may re-enter the kitchen/sitting room and mime looking out a window toward the audience.)

ANNE. Oh, look. There's a tiny glimmer of daylight left. I can take one last glance at the beautiful garden, the orchard, the brook, the woods...It's as lovely as anything I ever imagined. *(Singing.)*

**I DREAMED THAT I LIVED HERE A LONG TIME AGO,
BUT DREAMS DON'T OFTEN COME TRUE, DO THEY?
I NEVER EXPECTED MY DREAMS TO COME TRUE.
WOULDN'T IT BE NICE IF THEY DID?**

**GREEN GABLES, I'LL LOVE YOU
WHEN MORNING IS NEW
AND EACH BLADE OF GRASS
IS A'SPARKLING WITH DEW.**

I'LL HEAR THE BROOK SINGING
ITS HAPPIEST TUNE
TO "WHAT IS SO RARE
AS A DAY IN JUNE?"

GREEN GABLES, I'LL LOVE YOU
WHEN EVENING IS OLD
AND SUNSET IS PAINTING
THE SKY RED AND GOLD.

NO MATTER IF I SHOULD
BE SENT FAR AWAY,
I'LL ALWAYS REMEMBER
THIS BEAUTIFUL DAY—
THIS BEAUTIFUL DAY!

(The lights fade on ANNE. A moment later a rooster is heard crowing as the scene shifts to a street in Avonlea. REV. BENTLEY and RACHEL enter from opposite sides and meet.)

REV. BENTLEY. Morning, Mrs. Lynde.

RACHEL. Reverend Bentley. I've been meaning to tell you that your sermon sounded rather familiar Sunday.

REV. BENTLEY. Truth to tell, it's the same one I delivered the week before. My memory isn't what it used to be.

RACHEL *(aside)*. Nor your sermons, either. *(Back to him.)* Good day, Reverend. *(REV. BENTLEY exits.)*

(MR. PHILLIPS, a schoolteacher, and PRISSY ANDREWS, an attractive student in her teens, enter. They laugh, walking closely together.)

RACHEL. Well, Mr. Phillips—*and* Priscilla Andrews. *(MR. PHILLIPS and PRISSY quickly put a bit of distance between themselves.)*

PRISSY *(a bit startled)*. Mrs. Lynde!

MR. PHILLIPS. We—I didn't expect to see anyone but the schoolchildren out this early in the morning.

RACHEL. That seems quite obvious. I'm on my way to the Cuthbert's to look over the new boy they adopted yesterday. He'll be going to your school, no doubt, Mr. Phillips.

MR. PHILLIPS. And he'll certainly be welcome, of course.

RACHEL *(pointedly)*. It's nice to see the teacher taking such a *close* interest in his students.

MR. PHILLIPS. Yes. I was just helping Prissy—Miss Andrews with her geometry.

RACHEL *(aside)*. How conscientious.

MR. PHILLIPS *(overdoing it, as they leave)*. Now, Miss Andrews, let us once again review the difference between an axiom and a postulate.

(He and PRISSY exit as two or more SCHOOLCHILDREN enter boisterously, accidentally jostling RACHEL, then exit.)

RACHEL *(scolding them)*. Children, children! *(To herself.)* Children. If I had it to do all over again, I'd only have ten instead of twelve.

(MUSIC #4: "PLAYOFF: RACHEL'S THEME")

(RACHEL exits. The scene returns to Green Gables. MARILLA enters calling back outside.)

MARILLA. We'll need more chicken feed by next week, Matthew. Better get two sacks this time.

(ANNE enters from her bedroom area.)

ANNE. Miss Cuthbert—

MARILLA. Morning, child.

ANNE. Oh, please, won't you please tell me if you're going to send me away or not? I can't bear not knowing any longer. I spent the first half of the night awake and worrying—and the second half asleep and dreaming—about lovely Green Gables.

MARILLA *(after a deep breath)*. Well, I suppose I might as well tell you. Matthew and I have decided to keep you. That is, if you'll try to be a good girl and show yourself grateful. *(ANNE stares at her in relief and disbelief, then sits and quietly begins to cry.)* Why, child, whatever is the matter?

ANNE. I'm crying. I don't know why. I'm glad as glad can be. I've never been happier. Can you tell me why I'm crying?

MARILLA. Maybe because you're all excited and worked up. I'm afraid you laugh *and* cry far too easily…Yes, you can stay here, and we'll try to do right by you. You'll have to go to school, you know. But it's only two weeks till summer vacation, so you can start in September.

ANNE. I'll try so hard to make you glad you have me. I promise. Now, what would you like me to call you? Miss Cuthbert? Or Aunt Marilla, maybe.

MARILLA. Well, I'm not your aunt, and "Miss Cuthbert" sounds kinda distant, so you can call me just plain Marilla. And Matthew's Matthew.

ANNE. Thank you, Miss—thank you—Marilla. Now that I have a home, do you think I'll ever have a bosom friend in Avonlea?

MARILLA. What kind of friend?

ANNE. A bosom friend. An intimate friend. A really kindred spirit to whom I can confide my innermost secrets.

MARILLA. Diana Barry's the nearest little girl. But her mother is a peculiar woman who won't let her play with just anybody. So, you try and make a good impression.

(MATTHEW enters carrying a basket of eggs.)

MATTHEW. Eggs are up.

ANNE *(rushes over and hugs him)*. Oh, Mr.—Matthew. Thank you for keeping me. Have you ever been so happy you laughed and cried at the same time?

MATTHEW *(enjoying her enthusiasm)*. Well now, I don't recollect I have.

(There is a knock at the door. MARILLA answers it and RACHEL enters.)

RACHEL. Morning, Marilla...Matthew. *(Seeing ANNE.)* Who's she? Where's the little boy?

MARILLA. The orphan asylum made a mistake. They sent her instead.

RACHEL. Well, you're going to send her back, of course.

MARILLA. No, we're going to keep her.

RACHEL. But you know nothing about her. And you with no experience raising—

MARILLA *(cutting her off)*. Anne, this is Mrs. Rachel Lynde, one of our closest friends. She lives on the next farm.

ANNE *(tentatively, under the scrutiny of RACHEL)*. Good morning...ma'am.

RACHEL. Well, they didn't pick you for your looks, that's certain. She's terribly skinny and homely, Marilla. Come here, child. Lawful heart, did anyone ever see such freckles. And hair as red as carrots. Come here I say. *(ANNE goes to her, pauses, then lets fly.)*

ANNE. How dare you call me skinny and ugly and freckled and red-headed! You are a rude, impolite woman. I hate you! I hate you! I hate you!

RACHEL. Well!

MARILLA. Anne!

ANNE. How would you like to be told you're fat and clumsy and probably haven't a spark of imagination? You've hurt my feelings and I'll never ever forgive you! *(She stomps away and exits toward her room.)*

RACHEL. Such a temper!

MARILLA. Anne, come back here and apologize at once!

RACHEL. I certainly don't envy you bringing up *that* child, Marilla.

MARILLA. She was very naughty, I'll admit. But you shouldn't have twitted her about her looks, Rachel.

RACHEL *(very indignant)*. Well!

MARILLA. She's never really been taught right from wrong. She'll learn. *(Calling toward ANNE's room.)* Anne, come here this instant!

RACHEL *(after a pause as both wait for ANNE)*. Well, it appears she has no intentions of apologizing. You needn't expect a visit from me anytime soon, Marilla. Good day. *(She exits in a huff.)*

MARILLA. Rachel! *(Again calling toward ANNE's room.)* Anne, I'm ashamed of you! Now you come down here this instant! *(Calling out the front door.)* Rachel! Don't go just yet! *(To MATTHEW.)* I've got to stop that woman before she spreads this episode all over Avonlea. Rachel! *(She exits. Very concerned, MATTHEW goes toward Anne's room.)*

MATTHEW. Anne? It's me, Anne—Matthew. I'm here by myself right now. Would you be willing to come down and talk to me for a minute? *(MATTHEW goes to a drawer and takes out his pipe.)*

(ANNE enters reluctantly.)

MATTHEW. Anne, I think you'd better apologize and get it over with when they come back.
ANNE *(incredulously)*. Apologize to Mrs. Lynde?
MATTHEW. Just smooth it over, so to speak.
ANNE *(after considering it)*. Well...I—I suppose I could do it for you, Mr.—Matthew. I am rather ashamed of myself for my lack of control. But it's so humiliating to apologize when the other person started it. Still...I'll gladly do it for you.
MATTHEW. Just smooth it over. *(Looking out the front door.)* Here they come back. Don't tell Marilla I said anything to you. She might think I was putting my oar in. *(He puts his pipe away and exits out the side.)*

(MARILLA and RACHEL enter.)

MARILLA. I'll see if I can get her to come down and—*(They see ANNE who sinks slowly to her knees. Her "apology" is sincere, but melodramatic as well.)*
ANNE. Oh, Mrs. Lynde, I'm so extremely sorry. I could never express my sorrow even if I used a whole dictionary. I've behaved badly toward you and disgraced my dear friends, Matthew and Marilla, who have let me stay at Green Gables even though I'm not a boy. And you did tell the truth. My hair is red, and I'm freckled and skinny and ugly. If you don't forgive me, it will inflict a lifetime of sorrow on a poor little orphan girl. *Please* say you'll for-

give me, Mrs. Lynde. *(RACHEL looks bewildered, MARILLA relieved.)*

RACHEL *(after a brief pause)*. There, there, get up, child. Of course, I forgive you. Maybe I was a little too hard on you anyway. Don't mind me. I tend to be a trifle outspoken. Anyway, I knew a girl once with hair as red as yours. But when she grew up, it turned to a real handsome auburn.

ANNE. Oh, Mrs. Lynde, you have given me hope. I'm sure I will be a much better person if my hair will only turn to auburn.

RACHEL *(to MARILLA)*. Maybe she *will* turn out all right after all, Marilla—especially now that she's come to live with civilized folks. *(To ANNE.)* In time, we might even come to get along with each other, young lady. If you take a notion, you can come visit me one of these days.

ANNE. Thank you, Mrs. Lynde.

RACHEL. Good day. *(She exits.)*

ANNE. I apologized pretty well, didn't I?

MARILLA. Maybe a bit too well.

ANNE. But I meant it. I really did. I spoke awfully bad to her. And I'd never do anything to purposely embarrass or hurt you or Matthew.

MARILLA. I believe that. But you're going to need lots of moral guidance—even more than we can provide. We'll get you started to Sunday School and church right away. Let's go up to your room and see what you've got to wear. If necessary, we'll ride into town after breakfast and buy you a Sunday dress.

ANNE. How wonderful! And on the way, I'll breathe in the glorious atmosphere of my new surroundings. I may not say a word the whole trip.

MARILLA. Thanks be to goodness for that. *(They exit toward ANNE's room.)*

(MUSIC #5: "JESUS LOVES ME"/"HAVE YOU HEARD?")

(The scene changes to a Sunday School classroom as MISS ROGERSON, the teacher, and several BOYS and GIRLS, including DIANA BARRY, GILBERT BLYTHE, JOSIE PYE and others enter.)

ALL.
> JESUS LOVES ME! THIS I KNOW,
> FOR THE BIBLE TELLS ME SO.
> LITTLE ONES TO HIM BELONG;
> THEY ARE WEAK BUT HE IS STRONG.
>
> YES, JESUS LOVES ME!
> YES, JESUS LOVES ME!
> YES, JESUS LOVES ME!
> THE BIBLE TELLS ME SO.

MISS ROGERSON *(speaking)*. Very good, boys and girls. Now please sit quietly until I come back. It's my turn to help Superintendent Bell count the morning offering today. *(She exits as ALL sit.)*

JOSIE. Have you heard about the orphan girl the Cuthberts adopted?

(The following lines may be sung by ALL or by individuals—or groups—as desired.)

ALL *(singing)*.
> HER PARENTS BOTH WERE TEACHERS.
> THEY DIED WHEN SHE WAS THREE DAYS OLD.
> SHE GREW UP IN AN ORPH'NAGE.
> NO ONE WOULD TAKE HER I(WE) AM(ARE) TOLD.

**ANNE OF GREEN GABLES,
ANNE OF GREEN GABLES,
ANNE OF GREEN GABLES,
THE TALK OF AVONLEA!**

**SHE HAS RED HAIR AND FRECKLES.
HER TEMPER STARTED QUITE A FEUD.
MIZ LYNDE SAID ANNE WAS UGLY,
AND ANNE SAID *SHE* WAS FAT AND RUDE!**

**ANNE OF GREEN GABLES,
ANNE OF GREEN GABLES,
ANNE OF GREEN GABLES,
THE TALK OF AVONLEA!**

**HER CLOTHES ARE NOT IN FASHION.
HER SKIRTS ARE NEVER FULL ENOUGH.
SHE HAS NO FRILLS OR RUFFLES.
HER SLEEVES ARE PLAIN AND HAVE NO PUFFS!**

(MISS ROGERSON enters unnoticed.)

DIANA *(speaking)*. Maybe we're not being fair. She could be a very nice person. *(Someone notices MISS ROGERSON and clears his throat, "Ahem." ALL see her and quickly sing.)*

ALL.
**YES, JESUS LOVES ME!
THE BIBLE TELLS ME SO.**

MISS ROGERSON *(speaking)*. Twelve dollars and 36 cents—a very generous collection. Now, we must hurry along. We have only a few minutes today because of the guest minister who'll be speaking at church. If you'll open your quarterlies—

(ANNE enters. She is wearing freshly picked flowers on her hat.)

MISS ROGERSON. Hello. You're late.

ANNE. I'm dreadfully sorry. I was waiting for Marilla, but she had a headache and couldn't come. So I had to find the way to church myself.

MISS ROGERSON. Dallying all the while, I see, by picking flowers.

ANNE. Yes. Roses and buttercups. Aren't they lovely? Although pink and yellow aren't becoming to me, I know. *(ALL except DIANA and GILBERT, who seems a bit taken by ANNE, snicker as ANNE sits.)*

MISS ROGERSON. Now, as I said—before we were interrupted—open your quarterlies to this Sunday's question page. *(ALL except ANNE, who has no quarterly, do so.)* But do *not* look at the answers.

ALL *(except ANNE)*. Yes, Miss Rogerson.

MISS ROGERSON. On which day did God create the fish and the fowls? *(ANNE's hand shoots up as the others search for the answer.)* Yes?

ANNE. On the fifth day God created the fish and the fowls.

MISS ROGERSON. That is correct. Where was Cain sent after he had slain his brother Abel? *(Again, ANNE quickly raises her hand as the others seem unsure of the answer.)* Yes?

ANNE. Cain was banished into the land of Nod to the east of the Garden of Eden.

MISS ROGERSON. That's right. Now, what punishment did God visit on the evil serpent? *(Once more ANNE immediately holds up her hand as the others flounder.)* All right. You again.

ANNE. The evil serpent was made to crawl on his belly and eat dust all the days of his life.

MISS ROGERSON *(to herself)*. And she doesn't even have a quarterly. *(To ANNE.)* Child, how long have you been studying the Bible?

ANNE. A week. Marilla's been teaching me.

MISS ROGERSON. You must be a fast learner.

ANNE. Marilla's a fast teacher.

MISS ROGERSON. The class is encouraged to memorize and recite scriptural passages. Do you know any?

ANNE. Not yet. But I promise by next week I'll have lots of scripture to recite.

MISS ROGERSON *(to herself)*. Probably the entire Old Testament. *(A church bell rings.)* Time for church. Oh, one other thing. Our Sunday School picnic was so successful in the spring, we're going to have another one this summer in Superintendent Bell's meadow. *(ALL react favorably.)* And *if* you promise to know the answers to next Sunday's questions—as well as our little orphan girl knew them today—I think I can persuade Mrs. Bell and Mrs. Lynde to make ice cream. *(The GIRLS applaud.) If* you know the answers.

ALL. Yes, Miss Rogerson.

MISS ROGERSON. Now, don't dally. Go immediately to your pews in church. I understand the guest minister is quite punctual. *(ALL except ANNE, who seems in a daze, and DIANA, who watches her intently, exit.)*

DIANA *(after a pause)*. You're going to be late for church.

ANNE *(dreamily)*. Ice cream. I've never tasted ice cream before.

Act I ANNE OF GREEN GABLES Page 33

DIANA. You will at the picnic. It's going to be near the pond where I live.

ANNE. Oh, the Lake of Shining Waters. You must be Diana Barry.

DIANA. I am.

ANNE *(gazing at her)*. Marilla said you were pretty, but you're actually beautiful.

DIANA *(embarrassed, but pleased)*. Oh...

ANNE. You are. Honestly. Oh, my name is Anne Shirley— spelled with an "e." I'd rather be called Cordelia, but Marilla says that would just confuse everybody.

DIANA *(extending her hand)*. I'm pleased to meet you, Anne.

ANNE *(as they shake, somewhat awkwardly)*. Oh, likewise, I'm sure. We live very near each other. I'm at Green Gables.

DIANA. I know. It'll be nice to have someone to play with. My sister—Minnie May—is too little.

ANNE. Then it's settled.

DIANA. What's settled?

ANNE. We can be bosom friends.

DIANA. I—suppose so.

ANNE. Will you swear to be my bosom friend forever and ever?

DIANA. It's dreadfully wicked to swear. Especially in a church.

ANNE. Not my kind of swearing. It just means promising solemnly.

DIANA. That's okay then. How do you do it?

ANNE. We join hands. *(They take each other's hands.)* I'll go first.

(MUSIC #6: "THE PLEDGE"/"AMAZING GRACE")

ANNE *(singing)*.
> I SOLEMNLY SWEAR TO BE FAITHFUL TO YOU,
> DIANA, MY BOSOM FRIEND.
> AS LONG AS SUN AND MOON ENDURE
> OUR FRIENDSHIP WILL NEVER END.

(Speaking.) Now you repeat it, and put my name in.

DIANA *(singing)*.	CHOIR *(softly, offstage)*.
I SOLEMNLY SWEAR	**AMAZING GRACE,**
TO BE FAITHFUL TO YOU,	**HOW SWEET THE SOUND**
ANNE SHIRLEY,	**THAT SAVED A WRETCH**
MY BOSOM FRIEND.	**LIKE ME.**

BOTH.	
AS LONG AS THE SUN	**I ONCE WAS LOST,**
AND MOON ENDURE	**BUT NOW AM FOUND,**
OUR FRIENDSHIP	**WAS BLIND BUT NOW**
WILL NEVER END.	**I SEE.**

DIANA *(speaking)*. I heard	CHOIR *(still softly)*.
you were a strange girl	**AMAZING GRACE**
Anne Shirley, but I think	**HOW SWEET THE SOUND**
I'm going to like you	**THAT SAVED A WRETCH**
real well.	**LIKE ME—**

(MISS ROGERSON enters.)

MISS ROGERSON. Girls, time for church, stop dallying.
ANNE. Oh, we weren't dallying, Miss Rogerson, we were only swearing.

	CHOIR *(in full volume).*
(MISS ROGERSON reacts	—I ONCE WAS LOST,
with shocked indignation	BUT NOW AM FOUND,
as she and the GIRLS exit.	WAS BLIND BUT NOW
The scene switches back to	I SEE.
Green Gables. MARILLA,	
dressed for "going out,"	
enters adjusting her hat.)	

MARILLA *(calling toward ANNE's room).* Hurry up, Anne. Your company will be here soon, and I've got to leave! *(She begins to take food from the cupboard and put it on the table.)*

ANNE'S VOICE *(offstage).* Coming, Marilla. I just need to tie my bow and put on my shoes.

MARILLA. You'd have been ready in plenty of time if you hadn't spent half the morning sitting on the woodpile talking to Matthew. *(To herself.)* Chattering a mile a minute and him taking in every word like a perfect ninny.

(ANNE enters breathlessly.)

ANNE. But I had to tell Matthew all about the Sunday School picnic we had yesterday—the ice cream and the games and how Diana and I beat Gilbert Blythe and Jimmy Glover in a three-legged race. Marilla, do I look okay?

MARILLA. As well as you should.

ANNE. Thank you for allowing me to wear my Sunday dress.

MARILLA. Against my better judgment.

ANNE. But you have to wear your best dress when you're entertaining your best friend. *(She examines the spread on the table.)* Oh, it's all perfectly elegant, Marilla. Strawberry preserves, fruitcake, cookies, ginger snaps...and I'll make the tea when Diana gets here.

MARILLA. I think there's some raspberry cordial left over from the church social. It should be on the second shelf of the cupboard. You can have that, too.

ANNE. Raspberry cordial! *(A horse whinny is heard outside.)*

RACHEL'S VOICE *(offstage)*. I'm here, Marilla!

MARILLA. Coming, Rachel! *(To ANNE.)* Now, you and Diana have a nice visit.

ANNE. Oh, thank you for letting me have her over, Marilla. You're very kind to me. *(She kisses MARILLA, who savors the moment, then pulls back.)*

MARILLA. There, there. Never mind your kissing nonsense. You'll please me most if you do what you're told.

RACHEL'S VOICE *(offstage)*. Time to go, Marilla!

MARILLA. Hold your horses, Rachel. I'm coming! *(To ANNE.)* After Diana leaves, you can get going on your patchwork. Maybe you can finish it tonight. *(She exits.)*

ANNE *(to herself)*. I hate patchwork. There's no imagination in it. I wish time went as fast when I'm sewing as it does when I'm playing with Diana. *(She surveys the room.)* Is everything ready? Seems to be. Oh, the raspberry cordial. *(She crosses to the cupboard and begins to search.)* Second shelf. Peaches. Preserves. No raspberry cordial. Oh, this must be it on the top shelf. *(She takes out the bottle and two glasses.)* And some glasses. *(She sets the bottle and glasses on the table.)*

(A knock is heard. ANNE opens the door, and DIANA enters. The girls go into a "high society" routine, beginning with a very formal handshake.)

ANNE. Good afternoon, Miss Barry.

DIANA. The same to you, Miss Shirley.
ANNE. How is your mother?
DIANA. Very well, thank you. And Miss Cuthbert?
ANNE. The same. She has accompanied Mrs. Lynde to the Ladies Aid Society this afternoon.
DIANA. And Mr. Cuthbert?
ANNE. He is hauling potatoes to the boat dock today.
DIANA. I trust the crop was good this year.
ANNE. Very productive, thank you. *(They can no longer continue the "act" as they burst into laughter.)*
DIANA. Don't you just love to talk elegant?
ANNE. Yes, it's so...elegant. *(They giggle.)*

(MUSIC #7: "KINDRED SPIRITS")

DIANA *(looking at the food)*. This is so much fun. I'm so glad we're friends.
ANNE. Oh, but we're much more than friends. We're—*(Singing.)*
KINDRED SPIRITS, KINDRED MINDS,

DIANA.
SHARING THOUGHTS OF KINDRED KINDS.

BOTH.
**WE ARE CLOSE AS FRIENDS CAN BE
WITH SIMILAR TELEPATHY.**

ANNE.
KINDRED SPIRITS, KINDRED HEARTS,

DIANA.
SHARING WORDS AS COUNTERPARTS.

BOTH.
> **WE ARE CLOSE AS FRIENDS CAN BE**
> **WITH EMPATHIZING SYMPATHY.**

DIANA.
> **KINDRED SPIRITS, KINDRED SOULS,**

ANNE.
> **SHARING DREAMS AND SHARING GOALS.**

BOTH.
> **WE ARE CLOSE AS FRIENDS CAN BE**
> **IN PERFECT HARMONY!**

(They laugh once more, then go to the table.)

ANNE. We have ever so much to eat and drink, Diana. And the very best treat is Marilla's homemade raspberry cordial. *(She pours a glass for DIANA who begins to drink.)* You have some first. I'll begin with the fruitcake. And after we've had our fill we'll have tea. *(They giggle again.)* Do you think Mr. Phillips will let us sit together when school begins?

DIANA. He just has to. And if we're lucky, we'll be right across from Gilbert Blythe.

ANNE. I see nothing special about Gilbert Blythe?

DIANA. But he's the handsomest and smartest boy in school. He teases the girls something terrible—torments our lives out. It's wonderful. *(She drinks more cordial.)*

ANNE. You've finished your cordial already. You must have some more. *(She pours another for DIANA, who drinks.)*

DIANA. It's the best raspberry cordial I ever drank. *(She continues to drink.)*

ANNE. Everything Marilla makes is the best. She's teaching me to cook, but it's all uphill. I start daydreaming and forget things—like when I forgot to put the flour in the cake, or the sugar in the shortbread. *(They laugh, DIANA quite loudly.)* And last week was the worst. We had a plum pudding with sauce, and some was left over, so Marilla told me to put it in the pantry and cover it. Well, I forgot all about covering the sauce, and, Diana, a mouse drowned in it!

DIANA *(laughs, uproariously, then finishes her cordial).* Imagine...a *mouse.* May I please have another?

ANNE. Of course. *(She pours the cordial, and DIANA immediately begins to drink.)* Well, I lifted the mouse out and threw it in the yard, but I forgot to tell Marilla about it. The next day, Mr. and Mrs. Chester Ross from Spenserville were here, and Marilla served the pudding and sauce to them. *(DIANA is near hysterics over this as she continues to drink.)* Of course, I shrieked out, "You mustn't use that pudding sauce. A mouse drowned in it!" *(She laughs.)* I'm afraid I'm such a trial for Marilla. *(DIANA has suddenly become very quiet. She rises unsteadily.)* Why, Diana, what is the matter?

DIANA. I don't feel very well. I think I'd better go home.

ANNE. But we haven't had our tea. Let me put the food away, and we'll have some tea.

DIANA. I must go home.

ANNE. Let me give you some fruitcake.

DIANA. Nooooo!

ANNE. Would you like to lie down in my room? Where do you feel bad?

DIANA. I'm very dizzy. I must go home.

ANNE. Oh, this is so disappointing. Here—I'll help you. *(She puts her arm around DIANA as they struggle to the door.)* Steady. You poor thing. You must be getting pneumonia or something. Steady. That's it. Perhaps some fresh air will help. *(They exit as DIANA emits a loud groan.)*

(MUSIC #7A: "PLAYOFF: KINDRED SPIRITS")

(The scene moves to the parlor of the Barry home. MRS. BARRY and ANNE enter with DIANA draped around them. DIANA's younger sister, MINNIE MAY, follows.)

ANNE *(in disbelief)*. Drunk?

MRS. BARRY. Drunk! Disgracefully and shamefully drunk! *(They set DIANA down.)*

ANNE. But she only had a few glasses of raspberry cordial.

MRS. BARRY. Raspberry cordial indeed! I know currant wine when I smell it. *(DIANA giggles.)*

ANNE. Wine? Oh, no. I must have gotten out the wrong bottle. Mrs. Barry, please forgive me. I didn't mean to intoxicate Diana. *(DIANA giggles again, then moans.)*

MINNIE MAY. Diana's drunk, Diana's drunk, Diana's drunk!

MRS. BARRY. Shush up, Minnie May! *(To ANNE.)* I don't think I want Diana to play with you anymore.

ANNE. Oh, Mrs. Barry—

MRS. BARRY. And you'd better cancel your plans to sit with Diana when school begins.

ANNE. Please, Mrs. Barry. This will surely cover my life with a dark cloud of woe.

DIANA. I think I'm going to be sick.

MRS. BARRY. Minnie May, help me get your sister to her bedroom. *(To ANNE.)* As for you, young lady, I don't think you are a fit girl for Diana to associate with. Now please take your big words and dramatic gestures home with you and behave yourself.

Act I ANNE OF GREEN GABLES Page 41

ANNE *(near tears)*. Yes, ma'am. *(She exits hurriedly as MRS. BARRY and MINNIE MAY struggle with DIANA.)*

DIANA. I don't *think* I'm going to be sick...I *know* I'm going to be sick. *(She begins to gag.)*

MINNIE MAY. Diana's drunk, Diana's drunk, Diana's drunk!

MRS. BARRY. Shush, Minnie May, shush! *(They exit.)*

(A moment later, a school bell is heard as the scene shifts to a schoolyard and classroom.)

(MUSIC #8: "SCHOOL DAYS")

(Several STUDENTS enter the schoolyard. They are involved in various activities and horseplay as they sing.)

ALL.
> SCHOOL DAYS, SCHOOL DAYS,
> DEAR OLD GOLDEN RULE DAYS.
> READIN' AN' WRITIN' AN' 'RITHMATIC
> TAUGHT TO THE TUNE OF THE HICK'RY STICK.

BOYS.
> YOU WERE MY QUEEN IN CALICO.

GIRLS.
> YOU WERE MY BASHFUL BAREFOOT BEAU,

ALL.
> AND YOU WROTE ON MY SLATE, "I LOVE YOU SO!"
> WHEN WE WERE A COUPLE OF KIDS.

JOSIE *(to CHARLIE who is pestering her)*. Charlie Sloane, stop that!

RUBY *(to JIMMY who is similarly bothering her)*. Get away from me, Jimmy Glover.

TILLIE. Why can't you boys act nice around us girls—like Moody MacPherson does.

JIMMY *(mockingly)*. Moody Spurgeon MacPherson is a nice boy because he's going to be a minister.

MOODY *(piously)*. That is my calling.

CHARLIE. Well, I'm going into politics and get elected to Parliament. So I don't have to be nice. *(He harasses JOSIE again.)*

JOSIE. Help! Cut it out!

JANE. Nobody's going to be anything if we're late coming in from recess. Mr. Phillips said we had to be seated by the second bell, or we'll be punished.

(ANNE enters.)

ANNE. Has anyone seen Diana? She always meets me at recess.

BESSIE. I saw her sitting under the big maple tree. I think she was writing something. *(Looking off in the distance.)* Oh, look at those boys scampering down from those spruces. Gilbert Blythe climbed the highest of all. Isn't he irresistible, Anne?

ANNE. He's handsome enough, but he shows off too much.

JANE. We're going to be late. Come on. *(ALL except ANNE begin to move toward the classroom.)*

RUBY. Hurry, Anne, before the second bell rings.

ANNE. I'm coming Ruby, but I've got to find—oh, here she is.

(DIANA enters the playground as the others, as well as GILBERT BLYTHE, PRISSY ANDREWS, and perhaps additional STUDENTS who were not at the playground, enter the classroom.)

ANNE. Diana, I've been looking everywhere for you. *(DIANA, downcast, does not respond.)* Since your mother won't let us sit together or play after school, recess is the only time we can visit. *(DIANA hands a note to ANNE, looks at her sadly, then goes into the classroom. The bell rings as ANNE opens the note, containing a bookmark, and reads.)* "Dear Anne, Mother says I'm not to play with you or talk to you even in school *or* recess."

(As ANNE continues reading, MR. PHILLIPS enters the classroom and moves among the students, quietly examining their work on slateboards.)

ANNE. "Please don't be cross with me, because I love you as much as ever. I miss you awfully to tell my secrets to. I made you a bookmarker out of red tissue paper. When you look at it, remember me. Your true friend, Diana Barry." *(ANNE suddenly realizes she is late and tries to sneak into the classroom. She almost reaches her seat but is discovered.)*

MR. PHILLIPS. Anne Shirley, you are tardy. Perhaps you will be more punctual in the future if I have you sit with— *(He looks about the room.)*—Gilbert Blythe, who is occasionally late himself.

BESSIE *(aside)*. I wish he'd punish me that way. *(ANNE very reluctantly takes her slate and chalk and sits next to GILBERT who is pleased. Snickers and giggles fill the classroom.)*

MR. PHILLIPS. Quiet, everyone. Let me remind you while it is still early in the year that you must study hard at all times. Whether you finish school at Avonlea this year—or next—or beyond that—your ultimate goal is to pass the entrance examinations to Queen's Academy in Charlottetown. Who knows—perhaps one day an Avonlea student may win the coveted Queen's gold medal—or better yet, the Avery Scholarship. *(A pause.)* Now, work on your fractions.

RUBY. Will you check our work, Mr. Phillips?

MR. PHILLIPS. Later, Ruby. At the moment I must help Prissy—uh, Priscilla Andrews. She will soon be taking the Queen's examinations herself. *(ALL work busily as MR. PHILLIPS sits beside PRISSY and works with her.)*

JOSIE *(whispering across to ANNE)*. Anne, you're actually getting to sit with Gilbert Blythe. What kind of punishment is that?

ANNE *(whispering back)*. The *worst* kind. *(GILBERT laughs under his breath and tries to tickle ANNE. Through clinched teeth.)* Stop it! *(Giggles from around the room.)*

MR. PHILLIPS. Quiet, please! *(GILBERT takes ANNE's slate and keeps it away from her. She finally takes his slate and begins to do her work on it. Very quietly and deftly, without her noticing, he takes the ends of her braids and holds them outstretched.)*

GILBERT *(whispering loudly)*. Carrots! Carrots! *(Amid more laughter, an inflamed ANNE leaps to her feet.)*

ANNE. How dare you! *(She breaks the slate cleanly over GILBERT's head, the broken pieces dropping to the floor. The BOYS, especially, find this action hilarious. MR. PHILLIPS rises angrily.)*

MR. PHILLIPS. Anne Shirley, what does this mean?

GILBERT *(quickly)*. It was my fault, Mr. Phillips. I teased her.

Act I   ANNE OF GREEN GABLES   Page 45

MR. PHILLIPS. I am sorry to see a pupil of mine displaying such a temper.

GILBERT. Don't take it out on her, Mr. Phillips.

MR. PHILLIPS *(takes the slate from GILBERT and begins to write on it, reading as he writes).* "Ann Shirley Must Learn To Control Her Temper." *(He hands the slate to her.)* Now, you will stand in the corner and hold this slate above your head for all to see. *(Embarrassed beyond words and near tears, ANNE trudges to the corner. She holds the slate above her head so that the writing can be seen.)* Now, until I ring the bell, you may—if you have finished your fractions—talk quietly, *very* quietly, among yourselves. *(He resumes his place next to PRISSY. Loud whispering commences.)*

DIANA *(in great distress).* Poor Anne. I can't bear to watch her humiliation.

JOSIE *(matter-of-factly).* Her face is so white her freckles stand out like little red spots.

MOODY. I hope she didn't break Gilbert's brain. *(The BOYS snicker.)*

RUBY. I agree. Gilbert's the smartest student in school.

JANE. Anne looks so sad up there.

JOSIE. Well, it was her fault. She's too sensitive about her hair.

CHARLIE. You have to admit, Gilbert was mean to her.

JOSIE. I figured you'd take her part, Charlie Sloane. Everybody knows you're dead gone on Anne anyway.

CHARLIE. I am not.

JOSIE. My mother said your mother said you said Anne's the smartest person in class.

CHARLIE. Well, she is. She's smarter than Gilbert.

JIMMY. Then why is she standing in the corner and he's not? *(More giggling. During all of this, GILBERT seems very concerned over the situation, frequently glancing toward ANNE.)*

JOSIE. Well, maybe Anne is *somewhat* smart. But being good-looking is better than being intelligent. *(She preens for CHARLIE.)*

RUBY. I think Josie Pye's dead gone on *you,* Charlie Sloane.

CHARLIE. I'd rather be dead.

MR. PHILLIPS *(standing).* Quiet please! It is now time for the dismissal bell. When it rings, march out orderly. Do not rush. *(He exits as ALL gather their belongings and prepare to leave. GILBERT goes to ANNE. She turns away from him as the bell rings. He reluctantly exits with the others. Only ANNE and DIANA remain. DIANA puts her arm around ANNE and starts to speak.)*

ANNE. No, you mustn't speak to me, Diana. You must honor your mother's orders. *(A pause.)* Oh, I have been humiliated beyond belief. *(Looking at the slate.)* And look at this. Mr. Phillips left the "e" off my name! *(Gathering her belongings.)* That settles it. I'm never coming to school again. *(DIANA reacts in horror.)* Nobody—not even Marilla—can make me. Oh, Diana, now we won't ever see each other again. *(DIANA is near tears as ANNE sings.)*

(MUSIC #9: "FAREWELL")

ANNE.
**IN YEARS TO COME, THY MEMORY
WILL SHINE LIKE A STAR ABOVE.**

BOTH.
**FAREWELL, MY FRIEND, THOUGH WE MUST PART,
MY HEART IS YOURS WITH LOVE.**

Act I ANNE OF GREEN GABLES Page 47

(ANNE embraces DIANA who tearfully exits as GILBERT enters.)

GILBERT. I'm awfully sorry I made fun of your hair, Anne. Honest I am. Don't be mad at me for keeps. *(Handing her a small box of candy.)* Here's a candy heart for you. I brought it all the way back from New Brunswick. *(ANNE takes the box and drops it to the floor.)*

ANNE. I'll never forgive you, Gilbert Blythe! Never! *(She exits.)*

GILBERT *(calling after her)*. Anne!

(MUSIC #10: "ANNE OF GREEN GABLES")

(He slowly picks up the box of candy and repeats "Anne" to himself.)

GILBERT *(singing)*.
SHE HAS A FIERY TEMPER.
SHE LIKES TO HOLD A GRUDGE.
I'VE ASKED HER TO FORGIVE ME,
BUT SHE WON'T EVEN BUDGE.

SHE FEELS EXTREME EMOTIONS.
SHE'S EITHER UP OR DOWN.
SOMETIMES SHE PUTS ON HIGH-BORN AIRS.
SOMETIMES SHE'S JUST A CLOWN. *(He laughs.)*

SHE'S AWFULLY ABSENT-MINDED.
HER THOUGHTS ARE MILES AWAY.
SHE DREAMS THAT SHE'S A PRINCESS
WHO'LL BE A QUEEN SOMEDAY.

AT PICNICS SHE'S A TOMBOY.
SHE WON THE THREE-LEGGED RACE.
I THINK SOMEONE SHOULD TELL HER THAT,
FOR GIRLS, THAT'S OUT OF PLACE.

SHE'S OVERLY AMBITIOUS.
SHE HAS TO BE THE BEST.
SHE STUDIES HARD TO BEAT ME,
AND WE BEAT ALL THE REST!

SHE TALKS AND TALKS AND TALKS AND TALKS
AND SAYS WHAT'S ON HER MIND.
SHE NEVER STOPS TO LISTEN, THOUGH.
SHE'S NEVER SO INCLINED.

(Speaking.) But come to think of it—
(Singing.)

I KNOW SHE'S OFTEN SPEECHLESS
WHEN LOOKING AT A TREE,
OR SOMETHING REALLY BEAUTIFUL
LIKE SUNSETS ON THE SEA.

HER EYES ARE WIDE WITH WONDER.
SHE BREATHES A LITTLE SIGH. *(He sighs.)*
I WISH SHE'D BE THAT WAY WITH ME,
ALL INNOCENT AND SHY.

SHE'S VERY INDEPENDENT.
SHE LIKES TO STAND ALONE.
IT SEEMS THAT SHE'S DETERMINED
TO MAKE IT ON HER OWN.

AND WHAT DO I ADMIRE MOST?
HER SPIRIT AND HER GRIT.

NO MATTER WHAT SHE PLANS TO DO,
I KNOW SHE'LL NEVER QUIT.

SOMEDAY I'LL TRY TO FIND A WAY
TO START ALL OVER AGAIN.
THEN SHE WILL BE A FRIEND TO ME,
AND I'LL BE HAPPY THEN—WITH—

ANNE OF GREEN GABLES,
A DOZEN GIRLS LIVING IN ONE.
THO' ONE WOULD BE LESS TROUBLESOME,
SHE WOULDN'T BE HALF AS MUCH FUN—AS
ANNE OF GREEN GABLES,
THE GIRL THAT IS SECOND TO NONE.
ANNE OF GREEN GABLES,
FOR ME SHE'S THE ONE! *(GILBERT exits.)*

(The scene changes back to Green Gables. There is a knock at the door. MATTHEW enters from the side and answers it. RACHEL enters.)

RACHEL. Is Marilla ready?

MATTHEW. She'll be down in a minute. She's just tending to Anne.

RACHEL. Is the little thing sick? If she is, it's probably over that business about quitting school. But I'm glad you took my advice and didn't make her go back.

MATTHEW. You think Anne will ever want to go back to school again?

RACHEL. Of course. Especially if we get a new teacher. I hear Mr. Phillips is finally resigning.

MATTHEW. Well, when she does go back, I'd like her to have a nice dress to wear—like the other girls.

RACHEL. Matthew Cuthbert, for once I agree with you. The way Marilla dresses that child is positively ridiculous.

MATTHEW. Maybe you could pick out a dress for her over at Blair's in Carmody. *(He offers some money to RACHEL.)* I'll give it to her as a Christmas present. Something real pretty.

RACHEL *(taking the money)*. If I can't find one I like, I'll make it myself.

MATTHEW. With them fluffy things on the sleeves—like the other girls wear.

RACHEL. Puffs. Of course. It'll be the latest fashion.

(MARILLA enters.)

MARILLA. Sorry to hold you up, Rachel. *(Calling upstairs.)* Anne, Mrs. Lynde's here. Come down and say goodbye to us. We'll be gone a couple of days.

RACHEL. You ought to come with us, Matthew. Half the town's going. Might be your only chance to see the Premier of Canada in person.

MARILLA. Matthew's not big on political rallies.

RACHEL. Maybe he's afraid I'll embarrass everybody when I ask the Premier why he won't give women the vote.

(ANNE enters wearing a large lace cap which completely covers her hair. She is a bit subdued.)

ANNE. Goodbye, Marilla…Mrs. Lynde. Have a nice trip to Charlottetown.

RACHEL. Lawful heart, child, what are you doing wearing that old granny cap? *(Quickly, to MARILLA.)* She doesn't have head lice, does she?

MARILLA. No, she's okay.

RACHEL. That's a relief. Come here, Anne, and let me see if your hair is turning auburn yet.

ANNE *(taking a step backward)*. No, it's still red.

MARILLA *(quickly)*. We better get going, Rachel. Anne, you and Matthew take care of each other, and I'll see you tomorrow night.

RACHEL. Marilla, is that a lock of loose hair on your coat? *(She takes a bit of hair from Marilla's coat.)* Lawful heart! It looks green.

MARILLA. Can't be, Rachel. No such thing as green hair. *(She and RACHEL exit. ANNE sits at the table and cries softly.)*

MATTHEW. There now, Anne, it's going to be all right.

ANNE. She'll spread it all over Avonlea. She saw my green hair.

MATTHEW. But she doesn't know where it came from.

ANNE. That peddler told me the dye would turn my hair black. I shouldn't have listened to him. He lied to me. But he sure told the truth when he said it wouldn't wash out.

MATTHEW. Well, Marilla did the right thing by cutting it off.

ANNE. Right down to the roots.

MATTHEW. It'll grow back.

ANNE. Redder than ever, I'll bet.

(A knock at the door. MATTHEW answers it. MISS SUSAN STACY, in her mid-20s, enters.)

MISS STACY. Mr. Cuthbert?
MATTHEW. That's right.
MISS STACY. I'm Miss Susan Stacy.
MATTHEW. Won't you sit down?

MISS STACY. No, thank you. I'm in rather a hurry since I'm calling on several families today—although a number seem to be on their way to Charlottetown. *(Crossing to ANNE.)* You must be Anne.

ANNE. Yes, Miss Stacy.

MISS STACY. I've heard a lot about you. Good things, I might add. *(A pause.)* I'll come straight to my business, Mr. Cuthbert. It is possible that the teaching position in Avonlea may become available next year.

ANNE *(enthusiastic)*. Mr. Phillips is leaving?

MISS STACY. It's not definite, but I've been encouraged to apply. I'm a Queen's graduate. I was second runner-up for the Queen's medal and a nominee for the Avery Scholarship. I don't say this to boast, but merely to state my qualifications.

MATTHEW. You sound qualified to me.

ANNE. Why don't you start right now?

MISS STACY *(laughing)*. Thank you for your votes of confidence. I like Avonlea, and I would like to teach here. But I want to teach students who have goals and ambitions beyond Avonlea. Would the brightest and best wish to continue at Queen's or a similar institution? Would the parents—or guardians—be willing to pay for their children's education at such a place? I certainly don't expect an answer from you now, but I would like you to think about it.

ANNE. Miss Stacy—I don't even go to school. But I might if you were the teacher.

MISS STACY. That wouldn't be until next year. You'll miss a lot if you stay out till then.

ANNE. I have my reasons for not going.

MISS STACY. I'm sure you do, but do those reasons outweigh your desire for knowledge—and the dreams that knowledge can bring?...I'm sorry, I've overstepped my

bounds. I enjoyed our brief visit. Good day, Mr. Cuthbert...Anne. I hope we meet again. *(She exits.)*
MATTHEW *(after a pause)*. I'd send you to a place like Queen's even if I had to hold up a bank to do it.
ANNE *(hugging him)*. Oh, Matthew.
MATTHEW. But I guess we could scrape enough together without resorting to robbery. 'Course, if you wanted to go to Queen's with your friends, you'd have to be getting back to school soon.
ANNE. That man humiliated me. Everybody laughed at me. I can't go back.
MATTHEW. I'd be mighty pleased if you passed them entrance examinations someday.
ANNE. I'll bet you'd be even more pleased if I won that gold medal—or especially the Avery Scholarship.
MATTHEW. I'd be mighty proud, of course. But the main thing is just to do your best—even when you don't feel like it. That'd make me the proudest.

(A moment later, an urgent knock is heard at the door. ANNE answers it. DIANA enters breathlessly.)

ANNE *(delighted to see her)*. Diana! Did your mother say we can play together again?
DIANA. Mother and Father went to Charlottetown yesterday. They're staying with my Aunt Josephine till tomorrow.
ANNE. Diana, I'm overjoyed to see you, but you shouldn't disobey your mother while she's gone.
DIANA *(with alarm)*. It's Minnie May. She's awful sick. The French girl—Mary Jo—is staying with us, and she says Minnie May has pneumonia and the croup. But Mary Jo doesn't know what to do. And I don't either. *(ANNE looks at MATTHEW.)*

MATTHEW. I never took care of a young one before.

ANNE. I have. At the orphanage we had to take care of each other lots of times. I once helped a pair of twins through a horrible sick spell.

MATTHEW. Anne, you go with Diana. I'll fetch the doctor in Avonlea.

DIANA. I think he went to Charlottetown like everybody else.

MATTHEW. Then I'll go to Carmody and look for a doctor if I have to. *(He begins to put on his coat, cap, gloves, etc.)*

ANNE *(throwing on a coat)*. Matthew will find somebody. *(Going to the cupboard and taking out a bottle.)* I'll take this bottle of ipecac in case you don't have any at home.

DIANA. Hurry, Anne. Minnie May is coughing something terrible, and she looks just awful. I'm afraid she may be dying.

ANNE. We won't let her die. Come on. *(They exit.)*

MATTHEW *(to himself)*. What if I can't find a doctor?... Anne will just have to handle things herself. Hope that little girl's gonna be okay. The Watsons lost their youngest to pneumonia just about this time a year ago. *(He takes his pipe from the cupboard.)* A sad, sad thing. *(He exits.)*

(Music #11: "PLAYOFF: GOD'S IN HIS HEAVEN")

(The scene moves to the parlor of the Barry home. ANNE, DIANA and MARY JO, a French-Canadian girl in her late teens, enter carrying MINNIE MAY who is in night clothes. She is coughing violently and appears barely conscious.)

ANNE. I think she'll do better in here where it's warmer. The bedroom is too cold. *(They lay MINNIE MAY on a couch or bench.)* Diana, get me a spoon for the ipecac. *(DIANA exits hurriedly.)* We need lots of hot water. Mary Jo, put plenty of wood in the kitchen stove.

Act I   ANNE OF GREEN GABLES   Page 55

MARY JO *(nervously, with an accent).* Yes, right away. I'll do the best I can.

(She exits as DIANA re-enters with a spoon which she gives to ANNE.)

ANNE. Diana, get some soft flannel cloths. Do you know where they are?

DIANA *(very worried).* Yes. No. I don't know.

ANNE. Look in a bottom drawer somewhere. Mothers keep things like that in bottom drawers. *(MINNIE MAY emits a series of loud coughs.)*

DIANA *(crying).* Oh, Anne!

ANNE. Don't cry, Diana. She's going to be fine. I've seen lots worse than this. Now go get some cloths.

DIANA. Okay. *(She exits. MINNIE MAY coughs again and moans. ANNE feels her forehead.)*

ANNE *(very concerned).* She's sicker than anybody I've ever seen. A fever a mile high. *(She pours some ipecac into the spoon.)* Take this, Minnie May. *(MINNIE MAY is motionless. ANNE lifts her head.)* You've got to take every bit of this medicine. Wake up. Wake up, Minnie May! You've got to get rid of that phlegm. This will make you cough it up. *(She forces a spoonful down MINNIE MAY, who gags and coughs.)* Again. *(She feeds MINNIE MAY another spoonful. There are more coughs and moans.)* I've got to get all of this down you before the night is over. *(She stands over the listless MINNIE MAY.)* You poor thing. What you're going through is far worse than being humiliated at school, or getting your hair cut off, or losing your best friend. *(A pause.)* When this night is over, I'm going to put aside my petty pride and foolish vanity and go back to school. I'm going to pass those entrance examinations to

Queen's and aim for highest honors so Matthew and Marilla will be proud of me. The time for self-pity is over. *(Looking down.)* But first, Minnie May, we've got to get you through this awful crisis. *(More coughing and wheezing.)* Here, you've got to take more of this. *(She pours another spoonful of ipecac and works it into MINNIE MAY's mouth.)*

(DIANA enters with some cloths, and MARY JO enters with a steaming kettle.)

DIANA *(crying)*. Is she going to die?

ANNE. Not if we do all we can. And pray. I think there's a Bible verse that may help us through this.

(MUSIC #11A: "GOD'S IN HIS HEAVEN")

ANNE *(singing)*.
> IN TIME OF DISTRESS
> THE NIGHT MAY BE LONG.
> KEEP UP YOUR COURAGE;
> TRY TO BE STRONG.
> WE'LL WORK AND WE'LL PRAY
> TO KEEP DEATH AWAY, SAYING,
> "GOD'S IN HIS HEAVEN
> ALL'S RIGHT WITH THE WORLD."

ANNE, DIANA & MARY JO *(as they work with MINNIE MAY)*.
> "GOD'S IN HIS HEAVEN
> ALL'S RIGHT WITH THE WORLD."
> GOD'S IN HIS HEAVEN
> ALL'S RIGHT WITH THE WORLD."
> WE'LL WORK AND WE'LL PRAY

TO KEEP DEATH AWAY, SAYING,
"GOD'S IN HIS HEAVEN
ALL'S RIGHT WITH THE WORLD."

(MINNIE MAY coughs and seems to be clearing her throat.)

ANNE *(speaking)*. Good. Get that up. She's trying. *(Putting her hand on MINNIE MAY's forehead.)* And maybe—just maybe the fever is breaking. Diana, get more cloths. Mary Jo, get more wood. Hurry! Hurry! *(DIANA and MARY JO exit as ANNE calls after them.)* And keep saying that Bible verse over and over!

(ANNE continues working with MINNIE MAY. A moment later DIANA and MARY JO enter with cloths and wood respectively.)

ANNE, DIANA & MARY JO *(singing)*.
WE'LL WORK AND WE'LL PRAY
TO KEEP DEATH AWAY, SAYING,

"GOD'S IN HIS HEAVEN
ALL'S RIGHT WITH THE WORLD."

(They gather MINNIE MAY in their arms and form in a tableau.)

CHORUS *(offstage)*.
"GOD'S IN HIS HEAVEN
ALL'S RIGHT WITH THE WORLD."

CURTAIN—END OF ACT ONE

ACT TWO

(Music #12: "ENTR'ACTE: PRINCE EDWARD ISLAND")

SCENE: *The kitchen/sitting room of Green Gables.*

(Music #13: "DECK THE HALLS")

CAROLERS *(offstage, or coming down an aisle of the theatre, singing).*
> DECK THE HALLS WITH BOUGHS OF HOLLY,
> FA LA LA LA LA, LA LA LA LA.
> 'TIS THE SEASON TO BE JOLLY,
> FA LA LA LA LA, LA LA LA LA.
>
> DON WE NOW OUR GAY APPAREL,
> FA LA LA, LA LA LA, LA LA LA.
> TROLL THE ANCIENT YULETIDE CAROL,
> FA LA LA LA LA, LA LA LA LA.

(The CAROLERS repeat the first six lines softly—or hum—from "outside" as MARILLA enters from ANNE's room.)

MARILLA. Matthew, they're here! Bring that plate of cookies in.

(MATTHEW enters from another part of the house carrying the plate of cookies.)

MATTHEW. Well now, I'm coming. How does Anne look? *(He gives the plate to MARILLA.)*

MARILLA. You'll see soon enough. Now, let the folks in.

(MATTHEW opens the door as the CAROLERS—including MINNIE MAY, DIANA, MRS. BARRY, JOSIE, RUBY and GILBERT—enter.)

CAROLERS *(singing).*
**TROLL THE ANCIENT YULETIDE CAROL,
FA LA LA LA LA, LA LA LA LA.**
(They cheer and shake hands with—or bow and curtsy to—MARILLA and MATTHEW.)

MARILLA. That kind of singing deserves a reward. *(She offers the cookies to them. ALL, except MRS. BARRY, who politely declines, take one or two cookies each.)*

MRS. BARRY. We've had too many rewards already. At the Blythes, the Spurgeons, the Gillises, the Pyes, and we've got three more stops to make.

DIANA. Where's Anne?

MARILLA. Still getting ready.

DIANA. She has to look perfect tonight. She's the star of the program.

JOSIE. She's *one* of the stars. Ruby's reciting, too.

RUBY. And so is Gilbert.

MARILLA. Anne says you're singing a solo, Diana. And that you're real good.

DIANA. But not as good as Anne. When she recites "Curfew Shall Not Ring Tonight," it sends chills up and down my spine.

MARILLA. Well, she's been practicing it all over the house today. Didn't hardly have time to open her presents.

MRS. BARRY. Minnie May, did you bring Anne's gift?

MINNIE MAY. I left it out in the sleigh.

MRS. BARRY. Well, go get it. *(MINNIE MAY exits.)* We're mighty grateful to Anne. We have her to thank for Minnie May being with us this Christmas. The doctor said Anne saved her life.

MARILLA. Well, Anne was equally grateful when you came right over here and said she could play with Diana again.

RUBY. And they were sitting together the very next day.

JOSIE. When Anne came back to school, her hair made her look like a perfect scarecrow.

DIANA. Well, her hair sure grew back faster than a scarecrow's.

(ANNE enters wearing her new dress. She is radiant.)

ANNE. Merry Christmas, everybody! *(They return her greeting.)*

DIANA. Anne, your dress! It's beautiful. *(ALL agree.)*

ANNE. Matthew gave it to me. It's a perfect Christmas present.

(MINNIE MAY enters carrying a giftbox.)

MINNIE MAY. Anne—you've got puffs! *(ALL laugh.)* This is for you.

ANNE. Why, thank you, Minnie May. *(She opens the box and takes out a large bow.)*

MINNIE MAY. It's for your hair.

ANNE. It's lovely. And it even matches my dress. How did you know?

MRS. BARRY. Rachel Lynde was involved in the project. Need I say more? *(ALL laugh.)* Well, let's get going to the concert. We still have six more people to pick up. Hope we can fit them all in two buggies and a sleigh.

GILBERT. Would you like to ride in my rig, Anne?

ANNE *(a bit coolly).* No, thank you. I'll go with the Barrys.

MARILLA. Since Anne is spending the night with Diana, Matthew and I will go in our own buggy.

MRS. BARRY. Then we'll see you at the concert. *(ALL talk animatedly as they exit. MARILLA and MATTHEW begin putting on their coats.)*

MATTHEW. She looks awful pretty in that dress.

MARILLA. It was a nice present, Matthew, though I'm not sure she needed another dress. But she'll make a good impression when she's reciting tonight.

MATTHEW. She speaks her poetry real well.

MARILLA. She's a bright child, Matthew. I'm awful proud of her, but I'm not going to tell her so.

MATTHEW. Well, I'm proud of her, and I *did* tell her so. *(A pause, then "testing" MARILLA.)* I think she's smart enough to pass them entrance examinations to Queen's Academy...when the time comes.

MARILLA. Mrs. Barry said they were going to keep Diana in school right here at Avonlea.

MATTHEW. Queen's gives a mighty fine education.

MARILLA. For a mighty fine price.

MATTHEW. I reckon we could afford it somehow.

MARILLA. I'd miss her something terrible if she went away.

MATTHEW. But we have to do what's right by her.

MARILLA. Well, we don't have to think about it for a while.

MATTHEW. The time will come soon enough. We ought to keep our minds on it.

MARILLA. We better be going. We'll be far enough behind the carolers so that you won't have to join the singing.

MATTHEW. I got nothing against singing.

MARILLA. As long as there's nobody around to listen to you. Let's go. *(MATTHEW chuckles as they exit.)*

(Music #13A: "PLAYOFF: DECK THE HALLS")

(The scene moves to the Barry parlor. DIANA and ANNE enter.)

ANNE. It was a perfectly brilliant evening. Your solo was excellent, Diana.

DIANA. And your recitation was divine.

ANNE. The audience seemed to like all of us.

DIANA. Oh, Anne, isn't it wonderful that we can stay up as long as we like?

ANNE *(dramatically)*. "Curfew shall not ring tonight!" *(They laugh.)*

DIANA. Why don't we go to the bedroom and read. It'll be special since we get the *spare* room.

ANNE. Let's race and see who can get there first!

DIANA. All right.

ANNE. The first one to land on the bed is the winner.

DIANA. Then we'll put on our nightgowns and read far into the night. This is such fun.

ANNE. Get on your mark!

DIANA. Get set!

BOTH. Go! *(Giggling, they exit, running toward the bedroom.)*

(Suddenly a loud thump, followed by a painful groan, is heard. ANNE and DIANA re-enter in fear.)

DIANA. Merciful goodness!

ANNE. *What* was that? A ghost?

DIANA. Oh, Anne. I think it was my aunt Josephine Barry from Charlottetown. I had no idea she was here. She's old and rich and prim and proper. I'm sure she'll scold us dreadfully.

(AUNT JOSEPHINE, an elderly, cantankerous woman wearing night clothes, enters. She approaches DIANA.)

AUNT JOSEPHINE. There you are! You are the worst behaved girl I ever saw. Your parents ought to be ashamed for the way they've brought you up.

ANNE. But Miss Barry—

AUNT JOSEPHINE. Who are you? *(Back to DIANA.)* And another thing. I will *not* pay for your music lessons as I had promised your father.

ANNE. But Miss Barry—

AUNT JOSEPHINE. Who are you? *(To DIANA.)* And another thing. I will not stay two weeks as planned. I shall return to Charlottetown tomorrow.

ANNE. But Miss Barry—

AUNT JOSEPHINE. Who are you? *(To DIANA.)* And another thing…*(Back to ANNE.)* Who *are* you?

ANNE. Anne Shirley. I live at Green Gables. This was all my fault, Miss Barry—jumping on your bed like that. Diana is a very ladylike girl. You mustn't blame her.

AUNT JOSEPHINE. Oh, I mustn't, eh?

ANNE. It was only in fun. Please forgive us, Miss Barry. At least forgive Diana, and let her have her music lessons. If you must be cross with anyone, be cross with me. *(Gently playing the martyr.)* In my early days as an orphan, many people were cross with me. So I can endure it much better than Diana.

AUNT JOSEPHINE *(after a pause, somewhat placated).* Only in fun, you say?

ANNE. That's all. We had no idea you were in there.

AUNT JOSEPHINE *(after a pause)*. Well…I suppose I can take your word on it. You seem a truthful girl—and an interesting one at that.

(Music #14: "REPRISE: KINDRED SPIRITS")

ANNE. And you, Miss Barry, seem like a possible kindred spirit. Even if you don't look like one.

AUNT JOSEPHINE. I'm not quite sure I understand.

ANNE *(singing, as AUNT JOSEPHINE looks at her quizzically)*.
KINDRED SPIRITS, KINDRED MINDS,

DIANA.
SHARING THOUGHTS OF KINDRED KINDS.

BOTH.
WE ARE CLOSE AS FRIENDS CAN BE
WITH SIMILAR TELEPATHY.

ANNE *(as AUNT JOSEPHINE begins to understand)*.
KINDRED SPIRITS, KINDRED HEARTS,

DIANA.
SHARING WORDS AS COUNTERPARTS.

BOTH.
WE ARE CLOSE AS FRIENDS CAN BE
WITH EMPATHIZING SYMPATHY.

Act II   ANNE OF GREEN GABLES   Page 65

ALL.
> KINDRED SPIRITS, KINDRED SOULS,
> SHARING DREAMS AND SHARING GOALS.
> WE ARE CLOSE AS FRIENDS CAN BE
> IN PERFECT HARMONY!

AUNT JOSEPHINE *(to ANNE)*. You know, perhaps we can sit down sometime this week, and you can tell me something about yourself.

DIANA. Then you're not leaving in the morning, Aunt Josephine?

AUNT JOSEPHINE. No. I'll stay the whole two weeks. I want to be here for your first music lesson so I'll know if you're getting my money's worth. And maybe this Anne-girl will come over and talk to me occasionally.

ANNE. Of course I will, Miss Barry. *(AUNT JOSEPHINE exits, toddling toward the bedroom.)*

DIANA. Good-night, Aunt Josephine. *(The GIRLS give a deep sigh of relief.)* Thank you, Anne. I'll be eternally grateful.

ANNE. Well, it was my fault. Mrs. Lynde says I'm too impulsive. But when something flashes into your mind, it's so exciting, you just have to do it. If you stop to think it over, you spoil it all.

(MRS. BARRY, wearing a housecoat, enters.)

MRS. BARRY. Girls, you're still up. I forgot to tell you, Diana, your aunt Josephine came to visit while we were at the concert. Your father gave her the spare room, so you two will have to sleep with Minnie May. I think you should go to bed now. And for heaven's sake, don't wake up Aunt Josephine. She'd never forgive you if you did.

And, Diana, that might mean the end of your music lessons.

ANNE. Oh, we wouldn't dream of waking her, Mrs. Barry.

DIANA. Wouldn't dream of it at all.

(Music #14A: "PLAYOFF II: KINDRED SPIRITS")

(She and ANNE exit on exaggerated tiptoes as MRS. BARRY exits toward her bedroom. The scene changes to a street in Avonlea. MATTHEW and MARILLA enter and encounter RACHEL who enters from the other side.)

RACHEL. Why, Matthew and Marilla. What brings you to town on a harvesting day?

MARILLA. I'm dragging Matthew in to see the doctor. He's been a little short of breath lately. I'm worried about his heart.

MATTHEW. I'm all right.

RACHEL. Is Anne back from the exhibition in Charlottetown?

MARILLA. Mr. Barry's driving her and Diana back tonight. It was nice of Josephine Barry to let the girls stay with her.

RACHEL. I always thought that woman was an old sourpuss, but she sure took a shine to Anne.

MATTHEW. Well now, let's get this doctor business over with, Marilla.

RACHEL. Why don't you go ahead, Matthew. I need to talk to Marilla about a—a new recipe I'm trying out. She'll be right along. *(MATTHEW exits.)* Marilla, does Matthew still have his money in Abbot's Bank?

MARILLA. Every penny we've got.

RACHEL. I hear the bank's a little shaky. Mr. Abbot's getting awful old, and he's letting his nephews run the bank. You might think of putting your money someplace else.

MARILLA. I'll mention it to Matthew. Thank you, Rachel.

(She exits as REVEREND ALLAN and MRS. ALLAN enter on the other side.)

RACHEL. Well, the Reverend and Mrs. Allan.

REV. ALLAN. Good morning, Mrs....Mrs....

MRS. ALLAN. Lynde. Mrs. Rachel Lynde.

REV. ALLAN. I'm sorry. I'll have all the names before long.

MRS. ALLAN. I told my husband I'd memorize the congregation's names if he would memorize the Sunday sermons.

RACHEL. And very good ones they are, too. I miss Reverend Bentley's sermons, of course. But I had his memorized even before he retired. *(They laugh.)*

MRS. ALLAN. Let's see...The people you were just talking with...the Cuthberts?

RACHEL. Correct.

MRS. ALLAN. Their girl is in my Sunday School class. When I asked the pupils to tell their favorite Bible verse, Anne said hers was, "God's in his heaven—all's right with the world." I reminded her that the poet Robert Browning wrote that, but we both agreed it probably *should* be in the Bible. She's certainly a fine, intelligent young lady.

RACHEL. Of course she is. I practically raised her myself.

REV. ALLAN. We're very pleased to be in Avonlea, Mrs. Lynde.

RACHEL. Well, it's a new day in our town with all the comings and goings. We'll even have a new schoolteacher this fall. A woman of all things. I'm for giving women the vote, but I don't know if we ought to be giving them our schools. Of course, Canada's going to the dogs anyhow what with the way things are being run in Ottawa. But nobody asks me, so I just keep my thoughts to myself. Goodday, Reverend...Mrs. Allan.

(Music #15: "PLAYOFF II: RACHEL'S THEME")

REV. & MRS. ALLAN. Good day, Mrs. Lynde. *(The ALLANS exit in one direction as RACHEL exits in the other.)*

(The scene shifts to the Barry parlor.)

DIANA'S VOICE *(offstage)*. May we have our punch in the parlor, Mother?

MRS. BARRY'S VOICE *(offstage)*. Yes. If you promise not to spill it.

(DIANA enters, followed by others, including JANE, RUBY, GILBERT, JIMMY, ANNE, CARRIE, CHARLIE, MOODY and JOSIE.)

JANE. It's a wonderful party, Diana.

GILBERT. Your mother's a fine cook.

MOODY. The strawberry-rhubarb pie was delicious.

JOSIE. Which did you like better, Moody, the second or third slice you ate? *(ALL laugh.)*

DIANA. Actually, it was my father who made the strawberry-rhubarb pie.

ANNE. I think it's so imaginative when a man can cook.

RUBY. Diana, it was so nice of your parents to host an end-of-the-summer party.

CARRIE. I look forward to our new teacher next week.

Act II ANNE OF GREEN GABLES Page 69

JANE. Me, too.
JOSIE. Though it was a sad day when Mr. Phillips announced he was leaving.
CHARLIE. But not *too* sad.
RUBY. We girls all cried.
CARRIE. Quite convincingly, I thought. *(ALL laugh.)*
JIMMY. This has been such a great party, I can think of only one more thing that could make it perfect.
CARRIE. What's that, Jimmy Glover?
JIMMY. A small, friendly game of—"I Dare You"!

(Music #16: "I DARE YOU!")

ALL. Great idea! Let's do it! *(Etc.)*
JANE. Can we, Diana? Please!
DIANA *(a pause)*. I guess. I don't see what harm it could do. *(ALL cheer.)*

GILBERT *(pointing toward outside, singing)*.
I DARE YOU, JIMMY, TO CLIMB UP THAT TREE.

JIMMY.
GREEN CATERPILLARS WILL CRAWL UP MY KNEE!

ALL.
WE DOUBLE DARE YOU TO CLIMB UP THAT TREE.

JIMMY.
ALL RIGHT, I'LL DO IT. YOU CAN'T FRIGHTEN ME!

CHARLIE.
> I DARE YOU, MOODY, TO JUMP 'CROSS THE CREEK.

MOODY.
> I MAY NOT MAKE IT. MY CHANCES ARE BLEAK.

ALL.
> WE DOUBLE DARE YOU TO JUMP 'CROSS THE CREEK.

MOODY.
> BUT IF I FALL IN—

ALL.
> YOU'LL BE UP THE CREEK! *(They laugh.)*

CARRIE.
> I DARE YOU, JOSIE, TO WALK THE BOARD FENCE.

JOSIE.
> MY SHOES ARE SLIPP'RY. IT DOESN'T MAKE SENSE.

ALL.
> WE DOUBLE DARE YOU TO WALK THE BOARD FENCE.

JOSIE.
> OKAY, I'LL DO IT. I LIKE THE SUSPENSE!

ANNE *(speaking)*. That's nothing—*(Singing.)*
   I KNEW A GIRL ONCE WHO WALKED ON A ROOF.

JOSIE.
   I DARE YOU, ANNE SHIRLEY, TO WALK ON THE ROOF!

DIANA.
   DON'T DO IT, PLEASE, DON'T, FOR MY SAKE.

ANNE.
   I HAVE TO DO IT, MY HONOR'S AT STAKE!

DIANA *(speaking)*. No, Anne, it's too dangerous.

ANNE. Let's go do the dares. I'll even be the first! *(She exits as several of the OTHERS excitedly follow her with shouts of "Good," "She's going to do it," "I've got to see this," etc. MOODY, DIANA and JANE stay behind and look out the door—or window—and upward.)*

MOODY. She really is going to do it.

VOICE *(offstage)*. She's climbing up the drainpipe.

JANE. She's up on the roof.

VOICE *(offstage)*. She's taken your dare good and proper, Josie Pye.

DIANA *(calling out)*. Be careful, Anne! It's real steep up there!

VOICE *(offstage)*. Now she's *walking* on the roof. She's done it. *(ALL cheer.)*

DIANA *(calling out)*. Come down now, Anne!

VOICE *(offstage)*. She's starting to slip!

JANE. Oh, no!

VOICE *(offstage)*. She's starting to slide!

MOODY. Oh, no!

VOICE *(offstage)*. She's starting to fall!

DIANA, JANE & MOODY. Oh, no! *(They exit quickly as a loud crash followed by a muffled cry, is heard offstage.)*

(The scene returns to Green Gables. MARILLA enters, followed by MATTHEW.)

MATTHEW. I don't see a need for me to be here when she comes.

MARILLA. She'll only be here a little while. Anyway, there's something I need to talk to you about while we're waiting for her. There's some talk that the Abbot Bank is a little shaky.

MATTHEW. That's all it is...talk.

MARILLA. I'd feel better if we put what we got in the Savings Bank. *(There is a knock at the door.)* Just think about it, will you, Matthew?

(She opens the door, and MRS. ALLAN enters.)

MARILLA. Afternoon, Mrs. Allan.

MRS. ALLAN. Hello. And how are the Cuthberts today?

MARILLA. As well as could be expected. Have a seat. *(MRS. ALLAN sits as MARILLA calls towards ANNE's room.)* Anne, Mrs. Allan's here!

MRS. ALLAN. How is she managing these days?

MARILLA. Pretty good, I guess...under the circumstances. It sure perked her up when I told her you were coming. She even baked a layer cake special for you.

MRS. ALLAN. How thoughtful. *(MARILLA goes to the cupboard and takes out the cake, some dishes and forks and takes them to the table.)*

MARILLA. Later on, I know she'll want to show you her flower garden. *(She slices the cake onto the plates.)*
MRS. ALLAN. It's a fine girl you both are raising. I think the poet Browning describes her perfectly in his line: "The good stars met in your horoscope, made you of—"

(Music #17: "REPRISE: ANNE OF GREEN GABLES")

MRS. ALLAN. "—spirit and fire and dew."
MATTHEW. That's our Anne.

MRS. ALLAN *(singing).*
    ANNE OF GREEN GABLES, THE GIRL THAT WE LOVE,
    IS SPIRIT, FIRE AND DEW.
    LIVELY, BRILLIANT, FRESH AS THE MORNING
    WITH NO MISTAKES IN IT, OR FEW, HAS—

    ANNE OF GREEN GABLES,
    A DOZEN GIRLS LIVING IN ONE.
    THOUGH ONE WOULD BE LESS TROUBLESOME,
    SHE WOULDN'T BE HALF AS MUCH FUN.

    SHE FLIES ON THE WINGS OF ANTICIPATION,

MARILLA.
    OR WALKS IN THE DEPTHS OF DESPAIR,

MRS. ALLAN.
    OR FLOATS IN A DREAM OF IMAGINATION.

MARILLA.
    THE REAL WORLD FOR ANNE ISN'T THERE.

MATTHEW.
> BUT WHEN SHE GOES AWAY SOMEDAY,
> WE'LL FEEL A BIT OF A LULL.

MARILLA.
> AND WHEN SHE HAS A HOME OF HER OWN,
> THAT HOME WILL NEVER BE DULL WITH—

MRS. ALLAN, MARILLA & MATTHEW.
> ANNE OF GREEN GABLES,
> THE GIRL WHO IS SECOND TO NONE.
> ANNE OF GREEN GABLES
> FOR ME SHE'S THE ONE!

MATTHEW *(speaking)*. That's our Anne.

(ANNE enters. She has a large cast on her right leg and walks with a pair of homemade crutches.)

ANNE. Hello, Mrs. Allan.

MRS. ALLAN. Why, Anne. You're hardly handicapped at all.

ANNE. Matthew made this pair of crutches for me.

MARILLA. Well, let's eat.

MRS. ALLAN. I can hardly wait to taste your cake, Anne. I'm honored that you made it for my visit. You know, I came today especially since it's the first day of school, and I thought you might be a little down in the dumps.

ANNE. That's very thoughtful, Mrs. Allan. *(ALL except ANNE begin to eat their cake.)* But I won't miss too much school. My cast will come off in just two more weeks. Miss Stacy—she's our new teacher—said she would try to drop off my assignments before I start back. *(A pause as*

Act II   ANNE OF GREEN GABLES   Page 75

the three cake-eaters chew slowly and swallow hard.) Is something wrong?

MARILLA *(grimacing).* Mrs. Allan, don't eat any more—not even to be nice. Anne Shirley, what on earth did you put in this cake?

ANNE *(alarmed).* Nothing but the recipe. What's wrong?

MARILLA. It's horrible. Taste it yourself. *(ANNE tastes a small bite, then spits it into a napkin.)* What flavoring did you use?

ANNE. Vanilla. Just vanilla. There's the bottle right in the cupboard.

MARILLA *(getting the bottle).* Mercy on us, Anne. You've flavored that cake with anodyne liniment.

ANNE. Liniment?

MARILLA. I broke the liniment bottle last week and poured what was left in this old vanilla bottle. I suppose it's partly my fault, but couldn't you smell the liniment?

ANNE *(very upset).* No, I couldn't. I was still getting over my summer cold. Oh, Mrs. Allan, can you ever forgive me?

MRS. ALLAN *(putting her arm around ANNE).* There's nothing to forgive, my dear. I appreciate your thoughtfulness just as much as if the cake had turned out all right. Now, you mustn't feel bad.

ANNE *(a little brighter).* Well, this is certainly a new one for me. I do make lots of mistakes, Mrs. Allan. But there's one encouraging thing: I never make the same mistake twice. *(ALL laugh.)*

MARILLA. Matthew, we'll feed what's left of this cake to the pigs.

MRS. ALLAN. Anne, I'm very eager to see your flower garden. Why don't you show it to me.

ANNE. All right. *(MARILLA, carrying the cake, and MATTHEW exit out the side as MRS. ALLAN and ANNE go toward the front door.*) I love fall flowers the best. I think they're the most—

(*A knock at the door. ANNE answers and GILBERT enters. He carries a stack of books.*)

MRS. ALLAN. Gilbert Blythe.
GILBERT. Hello, Mrs. Allan...Anne.
ANNE (*somewhat coolly*). Good afternoon, Gilbert.
MRS. ALLAN. Anne, I'll go on ahead. You can join me later. (*She exits.*)
ANNE. Don't go, Mrs. Allan, I...(*To GILBERT.*) What are you doing here?
GILBERT. Miss Stacy let me bring your books and assignments to you.
ANNE. Why did you want to do that?
GILBERT. Maybe it's because I don't want you to have any excuses when I score higher than you on the Queen's entrance examinations.
ANNE. Perhaps you'll be the one looking for an excuse.
GILBERT. We'll see. Well...goodbye.
ANNE. Gilbert.
GILBERT. Yes?
ANNE. Thank you...very much.
GILBERT. Anne, has it ever occurred to you that we might possibly...be friends?
ANNE. It has...somewhat.

(*MARILLA enters, unseen by ANNE and GILBERT. Sizing up the situation, she quickly and quietly exits just offstage.*)

GILBERT. I'm awfully sorry I made fun of your hair that time. Besides, that was so long ago. I think your hair is awful pretty now. Honest I do. *(ANNE appears to be melting ever so slightly, but then a distant memory resurfaces, and a pained expression crosses her face.)*

ANNE. Carrots. You called me carrots! I can never be friends with you, Gilbert Blythe. Never!

GILBERT *(stung)*. All right. And I'll never ask you to be friends with me again, Anne Shirley. Goodbye. *(He exits.)*

ANNE *(to herself)*. Why did he really bring these books over? *(She puts the books away.)* Was it truly so that I won't have an excuse if he beats me on the Queen's exams?... Probably so. Well, *I'll* beat *you,* Gilbert Blythe. And when we're in school at Queen's, I'll study day and night to keep you from winning that gold medal!

(MARILLA clears her throat and enters.)

MARILLA. Did I hear Gilbert Blythe in here just now?

ANNE. He brought my schoolbooks.

MARILLA. He's turned into a right handsome fellow. He looks a lot like his father did at that age.

(Music #18: "MARILLA REGRETS")

ANNE. You knew Gilbert's father when he was young?

MARILLA. Oh, yes.

ANNE. What was he like back then?

MARILLA *(singing)*.
> JOHN BLYTHE WAS A NICE YOUNG MAN.
> MY FRIENDS CALLED HIM MY BEAU.
> HE USED TO BE SOMEONE SPECIAL TO ME,
> BUT THAT WAS SO LONG AGO.

**WE HAD A SPAT. DON'T REMEMBER JUST WHY.
THOUGH HE ASKED, STILL I WOULDN'T FORGIVE.
I MEANT TO—I WAITED TOO LONG.
I'LL REGRET IT AS LONG AS I LIVE.**

**I WISH I HAD FORGIVEN HIM
WHEN I HAD THE CHANCE.
YOU'D NEVER KNOW TO LOOK AT ME NOW,
BUT I ONCE HAD A BIT OF ROMANCE.**

(She smiles wistfully as ANNE puts her arm around her.)

MRS. ALLAN'S VOICE *(offstage)*. Anne, your chrysanthemums are lovely.

ANNE. Mrs. Allan. I forgot all about her. *(Calling outside.)* I'll be right out!...Thank you, Marilla. Thank you for telling me that. *(She and MARILLA exit in opposite directions.)*

(The scene changes to the Barry's parlor and simultaneously to a study room at Queen's Academy. DIANA enters the parlor reading a letter. JOSIE, RUBY, JANE, CHARLIE, MOODY and JIMMY enter the study room, deeply engrossed in books.)

ANNE'S VOICE* *(offstage, as DIANA silently reads)*. "Dearest Diana, Here it is Tuesday night, and I'm writing as I promised. I'm here at your aunt Josephine's. It was so kind of her to let me stay here while I take the Queen's examinations. We begin first thing in the morning. Everyone was

---

* *If ANNE'S VOICE cannot be amplified backstage, the entire letter should be read aloud by DIANA.*

frightfully nervous today, and the moods varied with the individuals."

RUBY. My hands are cold as ice. Feel my hands, Josie. *(JOSIE feels RUBY's hands.)*

CHARLIE. I think I'm going to fail algebra. I really think I am.

RUBY. I've been studying with Anne. She knows everything. I'm sure she'll do well.

JOSIE. Not as well as Gilbert.

JIMMY. I'll bet you a whole dollar that Anne scores higher than Gilbert.

MOODY *(who has silently been counting on his fingers)*. The Bible says we shouldn't bet.

JIMMY. Where does it say that?

MOODY *(barely audible)*. Twelve times six is 72, 12 times seven is 84, 12 times eight—

RUBY. Moody Spurgeon, what are you doing?

MOODY. Saying my multiplication tables. Twelve times nine is—

JANE. He's been saying them for three hours.

MOODY *(angrily)*. It steadies my nerves and makes me calm. Now don't interrupt! Twelve times 10 is 120, 12 times 11—*(His voice trails off.)*

DIANA *(reading)*. "Oh, Diana, if only the geometry examination were over. But as Mrs. Lynde would say, the sun will go on rising and setting whether I fail geometry or not. But I think I'd rather it *didn't* go on if I failed. I wish so much that you were with me. Yours devotedly, Anne."

MRS. BARRY'S VOICE *(offstage)*. Diana, come help me with the dishes. They won't wash themselves, you know.

DIANA. Coming, Mother. *(She glances back at the letter and manages a weak smile as she exits, fighting back tears.)*

(ANNE and GILBERT, both with their noses in books, enter, ignore each other, then exit. Note: GILBERT may remain on stage if desired. ALL continue studying. A moment later, MISS STACY enters.)

MISS STACY. Hello, everybody. *(ALL return her greeting.)* I'll be around to pick you up at your rooms early in the morning, so you should all get a good night's sleep. I know you wish to study all you can, but I recommend that you not work anymore tonight. Just relax and clear your heads. And I suggest that we end the day by going uptown for ice creams all around. My treat. *(ALL applaud and thank her as they start to leave.)*

(PROFESSOR ENGERRAND, a handsome man about Miss Stacy's age, enters.)

ENGERRAND. Excuse me, Miss Stacy—
MISS STACY. Philippe! I mean, Professor Engerrand. What are you doing here?
ENGERRAND. I heard you were in town with your class for the examinations. So, I had to come by and say, "*Bonjour, comment ça va?*"
MISS STACY. I'm so glad you did. Everyone, this is Professor Philippe Engerrand. We were students together here at Queen's. Now he's on the faculty. Some of you may be in his French class next year.
JOSIE *(quickly, holding up her hand)*. I'll sign up right now. I mean—*(ALL laugh as JOSIE turns away a bit embarrassed.)*
MISS STACY. Will you join us for ice cream, Professor Engerrand?

Act II ANNE OF GREEN GABLES Page 81

ENGERRAND. *Merci.* But before we go into Charlottetown, I suggest that you and I teach these students the one thing that all Queen's scholars must know.

CHARLIE. Oh, no. Not another lesson. *(The STUDENTS moan.)*

MOODY. What is it we have to learn now?

MISS STACY. A little relaxation exercise. Now, listen—

(Music #19: "THE CHARLOTTETOWN RAG")

MISS STACY *(singing).*
 WHEN YOU'RE FEELING TENSE,
 DON'T KNOW WHERE TO TURN,
 HERE'S A COMMON SENSE
 LESSON YOU CAN LEARN:

 TAKE A BIG BREATH, AND DON'T SAG;
 TAKE A BIG STEP AND DON'T DRAG;
 DANCE, DANCE, DANCE THE CHARLOTTETOWN
  RAG!

MISS STACY & ENGERRAND.
 CHOOSE A PARTNER, PLEASE.
 ANYONE WILL DO.
 STRUT AND WALK WITH EASE;
 POINT AND SIDE AND THROUGH.

 TAKE A BIG BREATH, AND DON'T SAG;
 TAKE A BIG STEP AND DON'T DRAG;
 DANCE, DANCE, DANCE THE CHARLOTTETOWN
  RAG! *(ALL dance.)*

ALL.
> **R-R-A-G!**
> **DANCE THE CHARLOTTETOWN RAG!**

ENGERRAND *(speaking)*. To the *salon de glace! (The STUDENTS look at him quizzically.)* To the ice cream parlor! *(The STUDENTS react with "Oh, yeah," "Right," etc., then cheer as ALL exit.)*

(Music #19A: "PLAYOFF: THE CHARLOTTETOWN RAG")

(The scene returns to Green Gables. ANNE enters carrying a suitcase.)

ANNE. Marilla...Matthew! I'm home! *(Looking about.)* Home. How lucky I am. I love you, Green Gables. Love you to pieces.

(MATTHEW enters.)

ANNE. And you too, Matthew! *(She rushes to him and hugs him.)*

MATTHEW. Well now, how did you get along?

ANNE. I don't know if I passed or not. I have this creepy, crawly feeling I didn't. But I'd rather not pass at all if I didn't come out ahead of Gil—of a certain somebody.

(MARILLA enters. ANNE embraces her.)

ANNE. Oh, Marilla. How I missed you. It seems I've been gone much longer than three days.

MARILLA. More like three years. *(She is delighted to see ANNE but tries to hide it.)* When will you know how you did?

ANNE. The pass list will be in the Charlottetown paper today, but we won't get it till tomorrow. Right now, though, I'm not even going to worry about it. I'm just going to enjoy seeing both of you. *(She hugs them. MARILLA turns away, a hand over her eyes.)* Marilla...what's wrong?

MATTHEW. Probably a headache.

MARILLA. No. It's not that. *(To ANNE, giving way slightly to her emotions.)* I...I just missed you, that's all. You've grown so tall...and stylish. You're even quieter now. I just wish you could have stayed the way you were...even with all your funny little ways. But you've changed.

ANNE *(affectionately)*. Not really. I've just...branched out a bit, that's all. *(Embracing MARILLA.)* No matter where I go or how much I change outwardly, I will always be your little Anne who will love you and Matthew and Green Gables more and better every day of my life.

MARILLA *(dabbing at her eyes with her apron)*. Now you've got me all mushy and silly-acting. Put on your everyday clothes, and help me feed the chickens.

ANNE *(laughing gently)*. I'd love nothing better.

DIANA'S VOICE *(offstage)*. Anne! Anne! Are you back yet?

(DIANA enters carrying a newspaper.)

ANNE. Diana! *(They embrace.)*

DIANA *(breathlessly)*. I'm sorry I didn't knock. I know it's impolite. But this is urgent. Look! *(She opens the paper.)* You passed!

ANNE. What?

DIANA *(as ALL gather around the paper).* Father brought the paper home from Bright River not minutes ago. He got it right off the train. Here's the pass list. You and Gilbert tied for first. And everybody from Avonlea passed. Miss Stacy will be so delighted. Moody Spurgeon got a conditional in history, and Josie Pye barely scraped by. But everyone passed, and your name is at the top of the list!

ANNE. Oh, Matthew...Marilla.

MATTHEW. Well now, I knew you could beat 'em all.

MARILLA. You've done pretty well, I must say.

DIANA. Oh, Anne, I got your letter. It was so exciting. You must tell me all about the trip.

ANNE. I've got to help Marilla feed the chickens.

MARILLA. Matthew can help me. You girls do your visiting and catch up on everything.

ANNE. Thank you, Marilla. Diana, come up to my room while I unpack. *(She takes the suitcase as she and DIANA go toward her room.)* Oh, you wouldn't have believed the English examination. My head was simply whirling, but after awhile I was finally able to—*(Her voice trails off as she and DIANA exit.)*

MATTHEW. Well now, I guess you did a fairly good job with her after all, Marilla.

MARILLA. Oh, go on.

MATTHEW. And me putting my oar in didn't hurt too much, I suppose. *(A pause.)* She's a smart thing. And pretty...and loving, too.

MARILLA. She is that.

MATTHEW. She's been a blessing to us, that's sure. There was never a luckier mistake than what Mrs. Spenser made...if it *was* luck. I think it was Providence—because the Almighty saw we needed her as much as she needed us.

Act II   ANNE OF GREEN GABLES   Page 85

MARILLA *(after a moment)*. Matthew Cuthbert, are you going to stand there gabbing all day or help me feed the chickens? *(They exit.)*

(Music #19B: "PLAYOFF II: THE CHARLOTTETOWN RAG")

(The scene changes to a parlor in a boarding house at Queen's academy.)

(JANE and RUBY enter, followed by JOSIE.)

RUBY. Josie, please hurry. It won't be daylight much longer.
JOSIE *(trying to fasten a necklace)*. Fine. Charlottetown is much more exciting after dark.
JANE. Why are you getting so fancied-up anyway?
RUBY. She hopes to see that French professor in town.
JOSIE. And why not? He's simply a duck...I need help with this necklace.

(ANNE enters.)

RUBY *(helping JOSIE with her necklace)*. Anne, are you coming?
ANNE. Not tonight. Miss Josephine Barry is picking me up in a few minutes. I'm spending the night with her.
RUBY. How nice. Remember how we all used to go home every weekend before Christmas?
JOSIE. We were so homesick then.
JANE. *And* we didn't have so much homework to do.
RUBY *(looking out a window)*. Oh, look, there's Gilbert on the front porch. He can walk us into town. Goodbye, Anne.
JANE. Have a nice time at Miss Barry's. *(She, RUBY and JOSIE exit.)*

ANNE. Thank you, I will.

(Music #20: "INCIDENTAL: GREEN GABLES")

(Smiles wistfully.) What was it Josie said? "We were so homesick then." Well, some of us still are. Matthew's probably coming in from the field about now. Marilla's probably making tea for him. They'll talk of the cows... the chickens...the crops...Will they talk about me? Do they miss me as much as I miss them?

(AUNT JOSEPHINE enters.)

AUNT JOSEPHINE. Anne-girl.

ANNE. Miss Barry! *(They embrace.)* I'm so glad I'm going home with you. Thank you for inviting me.

AUNT JOSEPHINE. Will you stay the whole weekend?

ANNE. Thank you, but final exams are right around the corner. And I must do well so I can graduate and get my teacher's license.

AUNT JOSEPHINE. Well, at least we can make the most of one night. I had my cook bake a fancy wild turkey with all the trimmings. How does that sound?

ANNE. Simply wonderful.

AUNT JOSEPHINE. Come now, the driver is waiting. *(They start to leave. AUNT JOSEPHINE stops.)* By the way, did I just see the Blythe boy on the porch?

ANNE. I think so.

AUNT JOSEPHINE. Nice young man. A good match for you, I'd think, Anne-girl.

ANNE. Well, now, I'm not so sure—

AUNT JOSEPHINE. *I* am. He's attractive. Seems studious, ambitious, *and* he possesses an even more important feature.

ANNE. What's that, Miss Barry?

AUNT JOSEPHINE. A strong chin. *(ANNE tries unsuccessfully to stifle a laugh.)* It's true. A strong chin is a man's most important attribute. *(She puts her arm around ANNE as they begin to leave.)* Now a man with a weak chin is as apt to leave you as he is to love you. When I was a girl about your age—*(Her voice trails off as they exit.)*

(Music #21: "PLAYOFF III: KINDRED SPIRITS")

(A train whistle—and perhaps a departing locomotive—is heard as the scene moves to a street in Charlottetown. MATTHEW, MARILLA and RACHEL enter carrying luggage.)

MATTHEW. I think it's this way.

MARILLA. Don't you know? You brought her to the academy.

MATTHEW. That was a year ago—and by buggy. We came by train this time.

MARILLA. Rachel, you've been to Charlottetown before.

RACHEL. Only to the fairgrounds and to hear the premier with you that time.

MATTHEW. I think maybe it's that way.

MARILLA. Well, if all else fails, we can always ask somebody.

(They start to leave as MISS STACY enters from the other side.)

MISS STACY. Miss Cuthbert! Mrs. Lynde! You're going the wrong way.

RACHEL. Miss Stacy—you're a beacon in the fog.

MARILLA. We haven't seen you since you left Avonlea.

MISS STACY. I wouldn't miss the graduation of the best students I've ever had. I only wish they could go on to college.

MATTHEW. We just wish we had the money for it. Queen's was about as much as we could handle.

MISS STACY. I understand the teaching position at Avonlea is vacant again.

RACHEL. Yes, and Gilbert Blythe has applied for headmaster. We haven't had a man since Mr. Phillips. Imagine me calling Gilbert a man.

(Music #22: "POMP AND CIRCUMSTANCE MARCH")

STUDENTS' VOICES *(offstage, singing).*
**COME, TAKE ON TOMORROW.
COME, CAST OFF TODAY.**

MISS STACY *(speaking).* Follow me. We don't want to be late. *(They exit.)*

(The scene shifts to a courtyard at Queen's Academy as the singing continues.)

STUDENTS' VOICES *(offstage, singing).*
**SUN BREAKS THROUGH THE SHADOWS
BRIGHT'NING OUR DAY.**

(Several GRADUATES, including ANNE and GILBERT, all of whom were the offstage voices, enter marching as they

sing. NOTE: If desired, the GRADUATES except for ANNE and GILBERT may remain offstage.)

STUDENTS *(singing).*
> **WE HAVE BUT ONE JOURNEY.
> IT COMES NOT AGAIN.
> LOOK WHERE WE ARE GOING,
> NOT WHERE WE HAVE BEEN!**
>
> **LOOK WHERE WE ARE GOING,
> NOT WHERE WE HAVE BEEN!**

(The PRESIDENT of Queen's enters and motions for the GRADUATES to sit.)

PRESIDENT *(addressing the GRADUATES and an unseen larger AUDIENCE).* Thank you again for your kind attention. As I mentioned inside at the official graduation ceremony, it is our custom to gather briefly outside here in the courtyard—prior to our reception—so that we might present what is traditionally our highest honor: the Queen's Academy gold medal. *(Applause.)* I am very pleased to announce this year's recipient—a student who has shown outstanding qualities—both personally and scholastically—from Avonlea, Prince Edward Island—Mr. Gilbert Blythe. *(Applause as GILBERT receives the medal from the PRESIDENT.)* Normally, this presentation would conclude our formal ceremony, but this year we are extremely honored to have another—equally prestigious—award to bestow upon one of our graduates. Because of our unusually high academic achievements this year, Queen's Academy has been awarded an Avery scholarship. It carries with it fully paid expenses for four years at Redmond College, leading to the bachelor of arts degree. I am extremely privileged to announce the recipient of this rare scholarship—a student who could not be more deserving—nor delightful, I might add. Again, from the village of Avonlea, Prince Edward Island—Miss Anne Shirley. *(Applause as the PRESIDENT presents an envelope to ANNE.)* And now we invite all of our friends, family and alumni to join the faculty and graduates for the reception and refreshments on the green. This year's graduation is now officially concluded. *(He exits amid applause. The GRADUATES embrace each other and congratulate ANNE and GILBERT.)*

GILBERT *(to ANNE)*. Congratulations, Miss Shirley.

ANNE. And the same to you, Mr. Blythe.

(Music #22A: "PLAYOFF: POMP AND CIRCUMSTANCE")

(They shake hands—not letting go for a moment—then exit in opposite directions. The other GRADUATES also begin to exit. The scene returns to Green Gables. MATTHEW and MARILLA enter carrying suitcases and set them down.)

MATTHEW. Well, it's nice to be back.

MARILLA. We've only been gone two days.

MATTHEW. Guess that's about as long as I've ever been away.

MARILLA. Well, I'm glad I finally talked you into getting a full-time hired man. Looks like he took care of things while we were gone.

MATTHEW *(picking up mail from a table)*. He even brought the mail in. Where's Anne?

MARILLA. Still gabbing with Diana, I reckon. It was nice that the Barrys let her come back with us.

Act II ANNE OF GREEN GABLES Page 91

ANNE'S VOICE *(offstage)*. Goodbye. I'll be right over as soon as I unpack!

(ANNE enters. She inhales deeply.)

ANNE. Oh, Green Gables. I've missed you so. I'm going to spend every minute memorizing you this summer before I go to Redmond.

MARILLA. I'll take your bags up to your room. You rest a little. You've earned it. To take a teaching license *and* that Avery scholarship all in one year...well, well.

ANNE. Why don't we all take a rest today?

MATTHEW. I dunno. There's always so much to do on a farm—even with a hired hand.

ANNE. I just wish I'd been the boy you sent for. I'd be able to help you so much this summer before I start to college.

MATTHEW. Well now, I'd rather have you than a dozen boys. I guess it wasn't a boy that took that scholarship, was it? It was a girl—my girl. My girl that I'm proud of. *(ANNE embraces him. He sits and looks through the mail as MARILLA picks up two suitcases.)*

ANNE. Here, Marilla. At least I can help you get these to my room. *(Taking a suitcase as they begin to leave.)* This one has all my books in it. Some of the students sold their books or gave them to friends, but I wouldn't part with a single, solitary one. *(They exit as MATTHEW looks intently at an envelope then hurriedly opens it and reads the letter inside.)*

MATTHEW. Well now. Well now...

(With a pained expression, he goes to a drawer and takes out his pipe. Suddenly he drops the pipe and letter and clutches his chest. He makes his way back to the table and

tries to steady himself. MARILLA and ANNE re-enter laughing and talking.)

ANNE. —then all the girls, except Josie, left, and there she was surrounded by all those—*(They see MATTHEW.)*—Marilla, look—

MARILLA. Matthew, what's wrong? *(They rush to him.)*

MATTHEW *(in great pain)*. It—it's the bank...the Abbot Bank. It failed.

ANNE *(softly)*. Oh, no.

MARILLA. Are you sure?

MATTHEW *(pointing to the letter)*. It's all right there. *(ANNE picks up the letter and pipe.)* Everything we had in the bank is gone. *(He groans.)*

MARILLA. Matthew, you've got to lie down. You're sick.

MATTHEW. I should have put our money in the Savings Bank like you said.

MARILLA. Well, you can't do anything about that now. Anyway, we didn't have that much.

MATTHEW. It's gone—all gone. *(He again clutches his chest and moans.)*

MARILLA. Matthew, is it your heart? *(He collapses.)*

ANNE. Matthew! *(She and MARILLA try to help him to his feet.)*

MARILLA. Anne, I'll get him to his room. You go get Martin, the hired man. Tell him to go for the doctor at once.

ANNE. Yes. Right away. And I'll get Mrs. Lynde and the Barrys and anyone else I can find. *(MARILLA struggles to get MATTHEW to his room. ANNE calls outside.)* Martin! Martin! It's Matthew—he's sick—real sick! *(She exits hurriedly as MARILLA exits holding MATTHEW.)*

(Music #23: "SHALL WE GATHER AT THE RIVER?")

VOICES *(offstage, singing).*
**SHALL WE GATHER AT THE RIVER,
WHERE BRIGHT ANGEL FEET HAVE TROD,**

(The scene changes to a road leading to a cemetery. TOWNSPEOPLE, who were the offstage voices, enter, perhaps carrying a simple wooden coffin, and cross slowly as they continue to sing.)

**WITH ITS CRYSTAL TIDE FOREVER
FLOWING BY THE THRONE OF GOD?**

**YES, WE'LL GATHER AT THE RIVER,
THE BEAUTIFUL, THE BEAUTIFUL RIVER,**
(They exit as the song concludes offstage.)
**GATHER WITH THE SAINTS AT THE RIVER
THAT FLOWS BY THE THRONE OF GOD.**

(The scene returns to Green Gables. ANNE enters. She carries the branch of a rosebush which she puts into a vase and sets on the table.)

MARILLA'S VOICE *(offstage).* Anne, is that you?
ANNE. Yes, Marilla.

(MARILLA enters from the side.)

MARILLA. You're going to be late for church. *(Gently.)* Where have you been?
ANNE. I left before you got up. I went to the cemetery and planted a rosebush at the foot of Matthew's grave—a white

scotch rosebush. He loved those roses the best. *(She slowly sits and begins to cry softly.)* Oh, Marilla. What will we do without him?

(Music #24: "MY LITTLE GIRL")

MARILLA *(sitting next to ANNE, taking her hand).* We'll just have to do with each other now. I don't know what I'd do if you weren't here. I hope you know I love you as much as Matthew did. *(She sings.)*

IT'S NEVER BEEN EASY TO SPEAK FROM THE HEART,
BUT YOU'VE BEEN MY COMFORT AND JOY FROM THE START.

YOU'RE MY LITTLE GIRL;
GOD SENT YOU TO ME.
IT WAS NOT A MISTAKE;
IT WAS MEANT TO BE.

I LOVE YOU AS MUCH
AS A CHILD OF MY OWN.
FLESH OF MY FLESH,
BONE OF MY BONE. *(ANNE hugs MARILLA.)*

YOU'RE MY LITTLE GIRL,
ANNE SHIRLEY, MY OWN.
I'VE LOVED YOU AND TAUGHT YOU,
AND NOW YOU ARE GROWN.

I'M GRATEFUL TO YOU
FOR ALL THAT YOU ARE.

Act II   ANNE OF GREEN GABLES   Page 95

**TO ME, YOU'RE MY BEACON,
MY BRIGHT SHINING STAR!**

(They embrace. A knock is heard at the door. MARILLA answers and MR. SADLER enters.)

MARILLA. Why, Mr. Sadler. I wasn't expecting you today.

MR. SADLER. Morning, Miss Cuthbert. I was just down from Carmody to visit my uncle here in Avonlea, and I thought we might talk.

MARILLA *(glancing uncomfortably at ANNE)*. Yes, I—we were just going to church.

MR. SADLER. Of course. Sunday isn't the most appropriate day to discuss business, anyway. I'll just drop by tomorrow. Morning to both of you. *(He exits.)*

ANNE. Marilla...

MARILLA. You'd best be getting ready for church.

ANNE. What did that man want? What kind of business?

MARILLA *(after a brief pause, fighting her emotions)*. I have to tell you sometime. It might as well be now. I've got to sell Green Gables. Mr. Sadler wants to buy it.

ANNE *(in disbelief)*. Sell...Green Gables?

MARILLA. We lost all our money when the bank failed. I had to let the hired man go yesterday. Rachel Lynde said I could board with her. I'm so thankful you're taken care of with that scholarship. I'm just sorry you won't have a home to come to on your vacations. *(She cries.)* Forgive me. Now it's my turn to cry.

ANNE. You mustn't sell Green Gables.

MARILLA. I can't stay here alone.

ANNE *(a pause, then with resolve)*. You won't be alone. I'll be here with you.

MARILLA. But you'll be at Redmond College.

ANNE *(firmly)*. I'm not going to Redmond.

MARILLA. Not going? What do you mean?

ANNE. Just what I said. I'm not going to take that scholarship.

MARILLA. Now, Anne, you can't—

ANNE. I'll get a teaching job, and we'll use part of my salary to pay a hired hand.

MARILLA. Where will you teach? Gilbert Blythe already has the position here in Avonlea. Anyplace else would be too far away for you to live here.

ANNE. Then I'll be the hired hand myself. I can do all the chores a man can do. Maybe even better. We'll be real cozy and happy here together—you and I.

MARILLA. I can't let you give up that scholarship.

ANNE. And I can't let you give up Green Gables.

MARILLA. But your dreams, Anne...your ambitions.

ANNE. They haven't changed. There'll be time for all that later on. You see, we've just come to a little bend in the road, that's all. And we just have to bend with it. *(A church bell is heard in the distance.)* Listen...church is about to start. We'd better go.

MARILLA *(hugging her)*. You blessed girl. *(A knock at the door.)* If that's Mr. Sadler, I'll just tell him—

(She opens the door. GILBERT enters.)

MARILLA. Why, Gilbert Blythe.

GILBERT. Morning, Miss Cuthbert.

MARILLA. We were just leaving, but...I'll go on ahead. I expect to see both of you at church. *(She and ANNE exchange smiles as she exits.)*

GILBERT. Hello, Anne.

ANNE. Gilbert.

Act II ANNE OF GREEN GABLES Page 97

GILBERT. I understand from Mrs. Lynde that you plan to sell the farm.
ANNE. Why does Avonlea need a newspaper when it has Rachel Lynde? *(They laugh.)* Marilla *was* going to sell. But not anymore.
GILBERT. Because you're going to stay here—and give up your scholarship.
ANNE. How did you know?
GILBERT. I know *you*—and your love for Green Gables. But how will you manage? You don't have a job, do you?
ANNE. I'll—find something.
GILBERT. How about the teaching job here in Avonlea?
ANNE. But that job is yours. I hear the board of trustees has already approved—
GILBERT. I withdrew my application.
ANNE. But why?
GILBERT. I...found a teaching job at White Sands. I recommended you for the position here. The board said all you need to do is apply.
ANNE *(very moved)*. Thank you. Thank you, Gilbert.

(Music #25: "INCIDENTAL: GOD'S IN HIS HEAVEN")

GILBERT. I hope after this we can be friends and that you'll forgive me my old faults.
ANNE. I forgave you long ago. I was just too stubborn to admit it.
GILBERT. May I walk you to church?
ANNE. Perhaps we'd better run. I think the service has already started.
GILBERT. It's too bad Mr. Phillips won't be there.
ANNE. Our old schoolteacher? Why him?
GILBERT. He might make us sit together for being late.

ANNE. Then let's pretend he *is* there, and we'll sit together anyway.

GILBERT. I have an idea. Why don't I reintroduce myself, and we'll start all over again.

ANNE. Excellent idea.

GILBERT. Hello...my name is Gilbert Blythe. I'm very pleased to meet you. *(He bows.)*

ANNE *(after a pause).* And my name is Anne Shirley, but please call me Cordelia. *(She and GILBERT smile at the memory of younger days.)* My name is Anne—Anne of Green Gables. And at this moment, God *is* in his heaven, and all's right with the world. *(She takes GILBERT's arm, and together they exit as the lights and music fade.)*

CURTAIN

(Music #26: "CURTAIN CALLS")

(ALL enter individually—or in groups—and bow. As ANNE enters, ALL except ANNE sing.)

ALL.
> ANNE OF GREEN GABLES,
> A DOZEN GIRLS LIVING IN ONE.
> THO' ONE WOULD BE LESS TROUBLESOME,
> SHE WOULDN'T BE HALF AS MUCH FUN—AS
> ANNE OF GREEN GABLES,
> THE GIRL THAT IS SECOND TO NONE.
> ANNE OF GREEN GABLES,
> FOR ME SHE'S THE ONE!

THE END

DIRECTOR'S NOTES

DIRECTOR'S NOTES

DIRECTOR'S NOTES

DIRECTOR'S NOTES

DIRECTOR'S NOTES

DIRECTOR'S NOTES

DIRECTOR'S NOTES

DIRECTOR'S NOTES